YEADON'S REGISTER

of

L N E R

LOCOMOTIVES

Volume Forty-Six Part B

Classes J50, J51, J84, J85, J93, N19 & M&GN 16A

Copyright Book Law Publications 2008
ISBN 978 1 899624 92 8

YEADON'S REGISTER OF L.N.E.R. LOCOMOTIVES - VOLUME 46B

EDITORS NOTE AND ACKNOWLEDGEMENTS

Welcome to the second Part of Volume 46 of *Yeadon's Register of LNER Locomotives,*where we cover the Gresley 0-6-0 side tanks of LNER Classes 50 and 51. As mentioned in Part A, we have also included the entire locomotive fleet of the East & West Yorkshire Union Railways along with the 0-6-0T classes of the Midland & Great Northern Railway for good measure.

The catalogue references for the locomotives featured in this volume are as follows:
DYE 1/47; DYE 1/48; DYE 1/52; DYE 1/61; DYE 2/6; DYE 2/7.

We would also like to acknowledge the contribution from the following photographers, most of whom, sadly, are no longer with us: I.C.Allen, J.W.Armstrong, R.J.Buckley, W.A.Camwell, H.C.Casserley, G.Coltas, A.J.Cook, R.C.Copeman, A.B.Crompton, A.W.Croughton, D.A.Dant, C.E.Dixon, A.G.Ellis, N.Fields, A.G.Forsyth, E.V.Fry, P.H.Groom, L.Hanson, T.G.Hepburn, B.H.Hilton, P.J.Hughes, W.M.J.Jackson, J.M.Jarvis, H.N.James, C.Lawson-Kerr, R.A.Panting, H.Percy, L.W.Perkins, L.R.Peters, P.Ransome-Wallis, S.J.Rhodes, J.Robertson, J.F.Robinson, C.L.Romane, C.J.B.Sanderson, E.E.Smith, J.L.Smith, Neville Stead, Rail Archive Stephenson, W.H.Tate, D.L.Wilkinson, P.Wilson, W.H.Whitworth, W.B.Yeadon.

Volume 47 of Yeadon's Register will present the North Eastern 0-6-0 tender engines.

The Yeadon Collection is available for inspection and anyone who wishes to inspect it should contact:-
The Archivist
Brynmor Jones Library
University of Hull
Hull
HU6 7RX
Tel: 01482-465265
A catalogue of the Yeadon collection is available.

First published in the United Kingdom by
BOOK LAW PUBLICATIONS 2008 in association with CHALLENGER
382 Carlton Hill, Nottingham, NG4 1JA.
Printed and bound by The Amadeus Press, Cleckheaton, West Yorkshire.

INTRODUCTION

General

In this volume we finish off our coverage of the Great Northern Railway 0-6-0T engines by highlighting H.N.Gresley's contribution - the J50 and J51 side tank classes. Because the opportunity arose, we have included a few of the 'odd' smaller classes which had a connection with either Doncaster or the Great Northern Railway. This then introduces for the first and only time in this series the complete coverage of the East & West Yorkshire Union Railways locomotive stock, appropriately in a volume dealing mainly with Doncaster maintained engines. The two former Midland & Great Northern classes were both 0-6-0 tank engine types and although not Doncaster maintained they had connections with the GNR by virtue of the joint ownership of the company.

Class J51

The thirty 0-6-0 side tanks which made up LNER Class J51 (GNR classification J23) at Grouping were all built at Doncaster during the period from January 1914 to the summer of 1919. Designed by Gresley, the class consisted of two batches with the first ten (157 series, LNER Class J51/1, later J50/1), coming into traffic from January to April 1914, having short coal bunkers whilst the later twenty (168 series, LNER Class J51/2, later J50/2), were turned out from December 1914 to June 1915 (10), and June to September 1919 (10), having longer bunkers. Numbered 157 to 164, 166 to 176, 178 and 211 to 220, the class was built to work the lines in the West Riding where stiff grades made good adhesion a necessity.

The boilers carried by the class had quite an interesting history of their own and the tale is a typical example of the GNR's thrift regarding locomotive matters.

The 4ft 2in. diameter boilers rendered surplus following the decision to rebuild the forty-one engines of Class R1 with the 4ft 8in type, produced a pool of far from life expired boilers that did not fit any other engines. Gresley decided to make use of them in his new design of 0-6-0 side tank. Altogether thirty-seven of these second hand boilers were modified for use in the thirty J51 class engines. The front ring of the boiler barrel had to be shortened by eleven inches, which resulted in the dome being well forward, distinguishing the J51 from the later J50 class. The domes were also much shorter resulting from their former use on Class R1 on which the boilers were not only pitched higher than on Class J51 but also had to conform to the restricted gauge of the Metropolitan Widened Lines.

Two of the J51 boilers (Nos.1388 and 1391) had three-ring barrels instead of the usual two, with the dome on the middle one. They had been ordered for fitting to Stirling single wheelers but instead had been used on Class R1 Nos.116 and 128 respectively, before passing to J51 Nos.3174 (April 1915 to October 1928) and 3178 (February 1924 to March 1934). Another boiler, No.872, was even older having been fitted to the single wheeler of that number in 1900. On this boiler the dome was further back than usual which was quite noticeable. After use on R1 No.117 it went to J51 3175 (January 1925 to October 1932). All three of these boilers had domes that were much taller than the others.

When all these second hand boilers became worn out, the thirty J51 class were given standard 4ft 5in. boilers and reclassified J50. This took place between March 1929 (No.3211) and March 1935 (No.3158). The replacement boilers were shorter than those previously carried and so did not extend so far back into the cabs. Fortunately the side tanks had originally been set 5ft 1¼in. apart and so did not require alteration to take the larger diameter boiler.

No.3167's boiler had been given a superheater when fitted in April 1914 and remained with that engine until it was rebuilt to Class J50 in October 1930.

Ramsbottom safety valves were fitted from the start but when rebuilt to J50 standard, Ross 'pops' started to appear on these engines.

All thirty were built with vacuum brake and no changes took place during their lifetime.

Class J50

When ten more of Gresley's 0-6-0 tanks were required in 1922 (Nos.221 to 230) the supply of boilers from Class R1 was deemed insufficient, so instead they were fitted with standard 4ft 5in. diameter boilers, but once again second hand. Ten more engines (Nos.3231 to 3240) were built in 1924 utilising previously used boilers. These twenty engines were separately classified J50 by the LNER although the GNR had classified them as J23 with the earlier engines. They were the last new engines to be built at Doncaster which did not receive new boilers at the time they were turned out. It will be seen therefore that the first fifty Gresley 0-6-0 tank engines all came out with boilers that had seen previous use on other classes.

The reason why surplus 4ft 5in. boilers were available for reuse was due to a programme of replacing these on classes D4 and J4 by 4ft 8in. boilers, coupled with the withdrawal of E1 class engines at that time, many of which were carrying quite young boilers. The 4ft 5in. boilers were also in use on classes C12, J55 and J57 tank engines and the Class J7 0-6-0s. Many boilers from these classes found their way onto Class J50, as well as being used for the rebuilding of Class J51. Eventually as time went by it was only classes C12, J4 and J50 that used these Diagram 11 boilers and there was much exchanging between classes C12 and J50.

Despite the fact that the J50 boiler was 3in. bigger in diameter than that used on Class J51, it was 13in. shorter in length (5in. less on the barrel and with a firebox 8in. shorter), so that the boiler did not protrude so far back into the cab. The domes were taller than on Class J51 and were set further back.

Renumbering of the Diagram 11 boilers by British Railways saw the following number blocks allocated:- 21800 to 21899 for those maintained by Doncaster and in existence at September 1950. No.21900 to 21924 was allocated to new boilers put into service from January 1951 to April 1953. Nos.21935 to 21939 covered the last new Diagram 11 boilers put into service between January and May 1957. Numbers 21940 to 21951 were an extension from No.21899 of the renumbering series, August 1953 to May 1954. Numbers 21925 to 21934 remained blank. Stratford works was given a separate series for the boilers on the J50s that they maintained. These were 21960 to 21966, used from February 1953 to July 1955. Cowlairs had their own series also - 21980 to 21987 - and these were allocated in the order of the age of the boiler on their books.

Nine engines, Nos.157 to 164 and 166, were built at Doncaster from January to March 1914 with short bunker, to which a cage was quickly fitted to augment coal capacity. They were classified J51 by the LNER.

The first ten engines which were to form the basis of Class J50, Nos.221 to 230, were built at Doncaster between October and December 1922. They were similar to the earlier J51 class except that Ivatt 4ft 5in. diameter boilers were fitted instead of the ex R1 class 4ft 2in. type. They were turned out in Great Northern grey paint with single white lining.

Class J50 was chosen as a Group Standard type by the LNER and fifty-two more were built between 1926 and 1939 (all with new boilers). The bulk of these LNER built engines were constructed at Doncaster but the last fourteen - numbered 599, 600, 602, 605, 606, 608, 611, 615, 584, 585, 587, 590, 595 and 598 in order of building - were turned out from Gorton between November 1938 and August 1939.

Design variations resulted in four class parts being required to cover all 102 eventual members of Class J50. The 1922 and 1924 built engines, totalling ten for each year, became J50 Part 2 whilst the thirty-eight built at Doncaster between March 1926 and April 1930 became Part 3. The Gorton engines became Part 4.

The class started out with vacuum brakes but all the engines built after Grouping up to 1930 had steam brakes fitted. Reversion to vacuum brakes took place with the fourteen engines built by Gorton.

Found mainly in the West Riding of Yorkshire, even towards the end of steam on BR, the class worked to the end in the place where it was intended to employ them. In 1924 when the twenty J50 class and thirty J51s were in service, they were all at work there. Ardsley had thirty-nine on its books, Bradford nine and Copley Hill, Leeds two. Their increased power over the saddletanks was a distinct advantage on the steep gradients that abounded in the area.

Further construction of Class J50 between 1926 and 1930 increased the total in the West Riding, but eight of the older engines were transferred to Immingham which shed later housed up to fifteen of the class until 1946 when they were displaced by J94 saddletanks. The Scottish Area received its first and only allocation of Class J50 in 1926 when seven new engines were sent to Eastfield. They remained in Scotland through to withdrawal, mostly at Eastfield but also at St Margarets and latterly a pair were at Polmadie.

By 1935, in addition to the above named sheds, Frodingham had six, Woodford Halse two and Stratford three. The final fourteen built in 1938-39 went to a variety of sheds, the class then appearing for the first time in the King's Cross District. On the eve of Nationalisation the class was distributed as follows:- Ardsley 25, Bradford 21, Copley Hill 7, Doncaster 15, Frodingham 6, Sheffield 3, Annesley 6, Colwick 2, Woodford Halse 3, Stratford 7, Eastfield 6, St Margarets 1.

It will be noticed that in LNER days none were allocated to the N.E.Area. However, in 1956 BR Regional boundary changes resulted in the West Riding District being transferred from ER to NER control. From 1958 onwards this led to the appearance of J50's at many of the Tees-side area sheds and also at Selby, Dairycoates and Goole. Beside the latter depot, former L&Y sheds at Wakefield, Low Moor and Mirfield received them too.

A major move had occured in 1952 when thirty J50s were sent to Hornsey where they displaced J52 and N1 tanks on the transfer trips to the Southern Region via the Widened Lines. The fact that they lacked condensing gear, hitherto regarded as essential for this work, was unaccountably ignored.

It will be seen that a comparatively small number of sheds saw long term usage of Class J50. There were of course other sheds which had one or more on their strength from time to time, such as Gorton, Trafford Park, Mexborough, Keadby, Tuxford, Leicester, Lincoln, New England, Neasden, and on the G.E. Section, Cambridge and Norwich - a case of when there was hard work to be done, send for a J50.

The 1946 LNER renumbering created the number block

8890 to 8991 for J50 class and all were duly renumbered in order of building. All of the class reached Nationalisation and duly got their BR numbering.

Withdrawals started in September 1958 and was completed five years later. During that period seven of the class were put into Departmental use after withdrawal and all of them lasted to at least May 1965. No.68961, as Departmental No.14 was the last to go in September 1965.

J84 (E&WYUR)

Of the three East & West Yorkshire Union Railways 4ft 0-6-0 saddle tanks taken over by the LNER in July 1923, Nos.1, 2 and 3, the latter engine was condemned two months after the event. The other two managed to continue working the colliery lines for which purpose the E&WYUR came into being.

Built by Manning, Wardle, Nos.1 and 2 followed each other into traffic in June and July 1895 respectively (works Nos.1307 and 1308). No.3 appeared from the same makers (works No.1489) some five years later and was, except for minor details, virtually identical to the earlier 0-6-0STs. The LNER classified them J84 and a duplication situation then arose because a class of ex North British Railway saddle tanks had also been allotted the same classification but, by the middle of June 1924 the Wheatley NBR engines had all been scrapped and the Yorkshire engines became the only J84 class. Class J85 (E&WYUR) [*see below*] was also duplicated with former NBR engines and it seems appropriate here to cast some light on the subject.

The reason why these two classes inherited by the LNER from the E&WYU on 1st July 1923 duplicated two classifications already in use on the NB section has always caused puzzlement. There was no other such instance on the LNER of two clases running at the same time with the same classification. Fortunately in the case of the E&WYU engines the duplication came to an end when the two ex NBR types were rendered extinct during 1924 by the withdrawal of J84 (14th June) and J85 (13th September).

The LNER classification system was drawn up in Doncaster drawing office during the summer of 1923 and reeived the approval of Gresley on 3rd September. It was based on information supplied by the other main workshops of the LNER. By the time information was obtained of the locomotives taken over on 1st July 1923 from the two small companys, the E&WYU and CV&K, it was too late to include them in the original scheme. The engines concerned, with the classifications later given them, were:-

Ex CV&H	2-4-2T F9	2 (8312), 3 (8313), 4.
	0-6-2T N18	5 (8314).
plus 0-4-2T No.1 withdrawn September 1923.		
Ex E&WYU	0-6-0T J84	1 (3112), 2 (3113), 3.
	0-6-0T J85	4 (3114).
	0-6-2T N19	5 (3115), 6.

Iy will be seen that the classification F9 followed the ex NER F8, but in the case of N18 and N19 a gap was left after the ex NBR N15 whereby N16 and N17 remained blank. There were already blanks in several other wheel arrangements to permit flexibility in the system for future construction or rebuilding. At that time the 2-4-2T type was not regarded as likely to be further developed, but both the 0-6-2T and 0-6-0T types were. So if it was thought necessary to allow for this by leaving N16 and N17 blank (the fresh acquisitions not being expected to last long in service), then equally in the 0-6-0T series currently ending with J91 it would be logical to leave J92 and J93 blank and give J94 and J95 to the E&WYU engines.

The likely explanation as to why they in fact became J84 and J85 would be due to a clerical error in a typed internal memo within the drawing office at Doncaster.

This became public when the first copies of the Engine Diagram Book and its accompanying Index, which listed individual engines and classes, was issued during May 1924. There were in fact two volumes - Tender and Tank. They had been compiled by the Doncaster drawing office staff from information supplied by the other workshops and were issued to the Locomotive Running Superintendents and other relevant officials. Numerous errors began to be reported, but it should be remembered that the people at Doncaster were not familiar with the locomotive stock on the other sections and could work only on the information that had been supplied to them by these sections.

As far as the duplicated classifications J84 and J85 were concerened, on the actual engine diagrams they were at least differentiated by the heading Section B in the case of Cowlairs classes and Section N (i.e. Doncaster maintenance) for the E&WYU pair. Similarly I the Index they fell under these same two separate sections.

The rest of 1925 was spent in sorting out problems with the Index in preparation for the next issue showing stock position as at 31st December 1924. It became apparent to Doncaster that the ex NBR J84 and J85 classes had become extinct during 1924 and reference to them could be deleted,as were their engine diagrams. Consequently it was decided that the E&WYU J84 and J85 classifications could remain as such.

During 1924 the surviving E&WYU pair, Nos.1 and 2, where given their LNER numbers 3112 and 3113 respectively. No.3 had been condemned in September 1923 and had not even been allotted an LNER number.

The boilers carried on the engines when the LNER inherited them, remained the only ones they were to carry and a Diagram number does not seem to have been issued by Doncaster. However, all three engines had been fitted with new boilers some years prior to Grouping after their original ones wore out.

When built the trio were all fitted with steam brakes only but in March 1904 No.1 had been fitted with a vacuum ejector to enable it to work, in conjunction with the Midland Railway, a short lived passenger service which had been introduced onto the E&WYU between Robin Hood and Leeds (Wellington) via the MR connection at Stourton. By the end of that year the service was abandoned but No.1 apparently kept the vacuum ejector until it got a new boiler in April 1914.

Even after the LNER took over, the 0-6-0STs continued working the colliery branches connected to their parent line until withdrawal. The former Great Northern shed at Ardsley became home after 1926 and Doncaster took care of their maintenance. Their seemingly long periods spent at 'The Plant' undergoing repair accounted for the fact that no spare boilers were available and the engines had to wait whilst their boilers went through the shops.

The first built was the last to be condemned, No.3112 succumbing in June 1930. Although Class J84 then became extinct, it is worth recalling that the E&WYUR and its colliery branches continued to supply the Nation with coal and for this purpose the LNER tried out many different saddle and side tank engines from the GNR, GCR, GER, and NER, including ex Hull & Barnsley 0-6-2Ts (N12). Tender engines sometimes helped out on the main line section during periods of intensive traffic. British Railways used J52 and later the J94 class, these latter engines working the branch to closure.

J85 (E&WYUR)

Like the three J84 tank engines, this solitary 0-6-0T became LNER property from 1st July 1923. Similarly it had been supplied by Manning, Wardle and was their works No.1398 of September 1898. Notes regarding class duplication are as above.

Numbered 4 by the E&WYUR, this engine was originally part of a trio of 0-6-2 tank engines (the other two were E&WYUR Nos.5 and 6 which became LNER Class N19) it was put to work from their Robin Hood shed where its usual duties consisted working the colliery branches. In April 1919 No.4 was rebuilt into an 0-6-0ST by Manning, Wardle and returned to work on the branch lines serving the collieries. Its coupled wheel diameter was three inches less than the 4ft 0in. wheels fitted to the J84 class which, although weighing virtually the same in working order, gave it an edge over those engines when hauling coal trains on the steeply inclined and somewhat dubious trackwork found on the colliery lines. Its favoured location was Newmarket Colliery and after Robin Hood engine shed closed in July 1926 it was allocated to nearby Ardsley shed from where it had easy access to the former E&WYU lines.

The LNER renumbered the 0-6-0ST 3114 in October 1925 during a General overhaul at Doncaster works. Withdrawn 20th February 1933, it was the last of the E&WYUR engines in existence.

J93

The nine Midland & Great Northern 'Shunting' Class 0-6-0T were inherited by the LNER on 1st October 1936, along with the rest of the M&GN locomotive stock. The engines had all been built at Melton Constable works at various times between October 1897 and May 1905 and, were numbered 98, 93, 96, 95, 15, 99, 97, 94 and 16 in order of building. In 1937/38 the LNER renumbered the nine by simply applying a '0' prefix and these were carried by most until the 1946 renumbering scheme took affect from August that year when four of the five remaining members of the class were numbered 8482 (098), 8484 (096), 8485 (095) and 8488 (094). The final engine to get the LNER 1946 number was No.16 which became 8489 in December 1946. None received their British Railways numbers although three survived into Nationalisation. They did not receive an LNER classification until July 1942 when they became Class J93. Those that received an overhaul at stratford after March 1938 even had the word 'Shunting' painted on the front bufferbeam.

Although built to the design of William Marriott, many aspects of the class were based on Midland Railway influences and even some of the boilers were made at Derby with the others constructed at Melton Constable. When the LNER took over their maintenance at Stratford, Diagram 46D was given to the boilers but no new ones were ever made by the LNER. The boilers then carried dated from 1927-30 when the whole class got new ones.

Braking was another area where MR practices were adopted and these 0-6-0Ts had steam brakes for engine braking with vacuum ejectors for train braking.

By the time all nine were in traffic, they had been dispersed throughout the M&GN system with two each at South Lynn, Norwich City and Yarmouth Beach, whilst Melton housed three of them. When the LNER took over things remained much the same except that South Lynn had four engines at the expense of Norwich which had been relegated to a sub shed and relied

East & West Yorkshire Union. This 9¼ mile long colliery line was absorbed by the LNER on 1st July 1923 and its engines numbered 1, 2 and 3 were given Class J84. No.3 was withdrawn on 6th September 1923, the LNER judging it not worth repairing. Nos.1 and 2 were built by Manning, Wardle & Co., Leeds in June and July 1895 and although No.1 remained as built, No.2 (shown here) had been rebuilt in April 1915 with deeper and thicker frames which were 6 inches longer at the front, both were classed J84.

E&WYUR No.4 was built in September 1898 by Manning, Wardle at Leeds as an 0-6-2T but in August 1919 they completely rebuilt it as an 0-6-0T and this single engine became Class J85. At rebuilding it got new 1¼ inch thick frames of similar profile to No.2. but the boiler dimensions were quite different hence its separate LNER classification. Note the different smokebox door and the shape of the front plate at the base. It got LNER livery as No.3114 when ex Doncaster 3rd October 1925.

The first engine of what was to become the J93 class was built in October 1897 at Melton Constable as Midland & Great Northern Railway No.14ᴀ. Renumbered 98 in 1907, it is seen here as taken over by the LNER from 1st October 1936. South Lynn, 23rd April 1933.

On 1st July 1923 two engines, No.5 and 6, were taken over from the East & West Yorkshire Union Railways. They had been built by Manning, Wardle & Co., Leeds in May and June 1899. No.6 had a very brief LNER existence because, due to a cracked frame, it was given no attention and on 6th September 1923 was withdrawn and broken up at Doncaster.

Built by Fox, Walker at Bristol in July 1877, No.16A was works shunter at Melton Constable. Although not withdrawn until 28th October 1937, it received neither LNER number nor classification. Note that it had no lamp irons on its front buffer beam, but it did carry them earlier. Note also the sloping front to the smokebox. Melton Constable.

on Melton Constable for its locomotive cover. Apart from the class visiting Stratford works for overhaul or scrapping, Nos.8485 and 8488 were surprisingly sent north to Darlington to be cut up in May 1948.

The first to be withdrawn by the LNER was No.097 in March 1943 followed by No.093 in June 1944. 1945 saw two J93 condemned but none went in 1946. During 1947 No.8482 was withdrawn in January and No.8485 followed in December. In January 1948 No.8488 was condemned and in May No.8484 went the same way leaving just No.8489 which survived until August 1949 working at Melton Constable.

M&GN No.16A

This engine was the survivor of a pair of 0-6-0 saddle tanks built by Fox, Walker & Co. in 1877 for the short lived Great Yarmouth & Stalham Light Railway. Long before the LNER had anything to do with the 0-6-0ST, it had gone through a numbers of ownership changes. In 1878 the GY&SLR changed its name to the Yarmouth & North Norfolk Light Railway which amalgamated with the Lynn & Fakenham and the Yarmouth Union on 1st January 1883 to form the Eastern & Midlands Railway. It was with this latter company that the engine first received a running number and its nameplate STALHAM was replaced by the number 16. Its twin became No.15 sans nameplate ORMESBY. In 1893 both engines became part of the newly created Midland & Great North Joint. In 1901 No.15 was withdrawn when a new 0-6-0T (LNER J93 No.015) was put into traffic by Melton works.

No.16 continued in employment at Melton but was put onto the M&GNR Duplicate List as early as May 1905 when another new 0-6-0 tank engine took its number. It then became 16A and remained so until withdrawn on 28th October 1937 during its only trip to Stratford.

N19

The two 0-6-2 saddle tanks numbered 5 and 6 by the E&WYUR completed the locomotive stock of that company handed over to the LNER. Both engines had been supplied by Manning, Wardle in 1899 specifically for working the coal trains on the railway. Originally there were three of these engines. No.4 was

---

M&GN 'FOX WALKER'
No LNER Classification.

Fox Walker 338.

To traffic 7/1877.

REPAIRS:
MC. ?/?—?/2/29.**G.**
MC. ?/?—?/11/34.**G.**
Str. ?/9/37. *Not repaired.*

BOILERS:
16.
16A *(new)* ?/2/29.

SHED:
Melton Constable works *at* 1/10/36.

WITHDRAWN: 28/10/37.
Cut up at Stratford.

---

the first to be supplied in 1898, but had been rebuilt by Manning, Wardle in 1919 as an 0-6-0 tank and is described herein under Class J85.

When taken over by the LNER No.6 was found to have a cracked frame and was withdrawn during the following September. No.5 however was in good working order and served its new master for a further five years. At the end of a three month long overhaul at Doncaster works which was completed in March 1925, it had been renumbered 3115 which, incidentally was the highest number achieved by the former E&WYUR fleet.

Like the rest of the coal hauling line's engines, the two 0-6-2STs were fitted with steam brakes and no change was made during their lifetime.

The first of the renumbered engines withdrawn by the LNER, No.3115 was condemned at Doncaster on 1st March 1928 and cut up shortly afterwards. Class N19 was extinct.

One engine, No.167 built at Doncaster in April 1914 as above but was fitted with a 16-element Robinson superheater for comparison purposes. The coal saving was only 3.7% so no more were done. Note the forward position of the chimney.

Ten more engines, Nos.168 to 176 and 178, were built at Doncaster from December 1914 to June 1915 similar to the previous batch but with a 4ft 2in. long bunker instead of 3ft 0⅝in. Except for No.173 no cage was fitted (*see* page 120, bottom). The cage on No.173 was removed in GNR days. Note the whistle does not project above the cab roof as it did on the earlier engines. The front of the tanks is 5½in. further back (*see* page 121, bottom) and the rear buffer beam is single steel plate instead of wooden sandwich type.

CLASS J 50 & J 51

3157

Doncaster 1414.

To traffic 1/1914.

REPAIRS:
Don. 29/9/20—26/2/21.**G.**
Don. 22/1—3/5/23.**G.**
Don. 2/6—1/9/26.**G.**
Don. 26/10—23/11/29.**G.**
Rebuilt to J50.
Don. 17/12/33—10/3/34.**G.**
Don. 31/12/37—8/1/38.**G.**
Don. 18/10—15/11/41.**G.**
Dar. 7—11/7/42.**L.**
En route to Doncaster.
Don. 15/7—24/8/42.**G.**
WD. 4/12/42—28/1/43.**L.**
At Stranraer.
WD. 17/9/43—25/3/44.**H.**
No.11 Mobile Workshop, Lef-fnoll.
Sent to Stranraer engine shed 29/6/45 for return to LNER.
Don. 1/10—2/11/45.**H.**
Don. 26/7—20/8/48.**G.**
Don. 11/5—8/6/53.**G.**
Don. 26/7—24/8/57.**G.**
Don. 10/3/61. *Not repaired.*

BOILERS:
6783 *(ex R1 142).*
6765 *(ex3172)* 1/9/26.
8311 *(new)* 23/11/29.
8325 *(ex3169)* 8/1/38.
9820 *(new)* 20/8/48.
21905 *(ex C12 67371)* 8/6/53.
21876 *(ex68981)* 24/8/57.

SHEDS:
Ardsley.
Copley Hill 9/1/28.
Ardsley 3/12/28.
Bradford 16/10/39.
Ardsley 23/12/39.
WD Cairnryan 11/7/42.
Immingham 12/8/45.
Frodingham 28/7/46.
Doncaster 26/9/46.
Mexborough 18/12/49.
Doncaster 15/10/50.
Hornsey 19/10/52.
Ardsley 23/11/52.

RENUMBERED:
3157 1/9/26.
3180 18/5/45. *By LNER rep.*
8890 8/12/46.
68890 20/8/48.

CONDEMNED: 20/3/61.
Cut up at Doncaster.

3158

Doncaster 1416.

To traffic 2/1914.

REPAIRS:
Don. ?/?—?/4/18.**G.**
Don. 26/8—30/10/20.**G.**
Don. 13/8—31/10/25. **G.**
Don. 1/10—17/11/28.**G.**
Don. 20/2—12/3/32.**G.**
Don. 23—30/3/35.**G.**
Rebuilt to J50.
Don. 18/3—22/4/39.**G.**
Don. 1—22/5/43.**G.**
Don. 19/10—6/11/46.**G.**
Green livery.
Don. 15/8—26/9/49.**G.**
Don. 30/6—24/7/52.**G.**
Str. 11/3—21/5/54.**C/L.**
Str. 21/5—1/8/57.**G.**
Don. 2—23/7/58.**C/H.**

BOILERS:
1621 *(ex R1 126).*
6788 *(ex R1 147)* ?/4/18.
6762 *(ex R1 132)* 17/11/28.
8149 *(ex J55 3918)* 30/3/35.
8511 *(ex3235)* 22/5/43.
8450 *(ex8931)* 26/9/49.
21874 *(reno from 9509)* 24/7/52.
21962 *(ex8920)* 1/8/57.
21820 *(ex68923)* 23/7/58.

SHEDS:
Ardsley.
Copley Hill 22/8/29.
Ardsley 18/10/29.
Copley Hill 13/6/33.
Ardsley 23/8/33.
Woodford Halse 11/12/40.
Colwick 19/6/49.
Hornsey 28/9/52.
King's Cross 9/7/61.

RENUMBERED:
3158 31/10/25.
3181 23/6/45.
8891 6/11/46.
68891 26/9/49.

CONDEMNED: 25/7/61.
Into Don. for cut up 27/7/61.

3159

Doncaster 1417.

To traffic 2/1914.

REPAIRS:
Don. 22/5—12/10/22.**G.**
Don. 1/9—5/12/25.**G.**
Don. 5/4—24/8/29.**G.**
Rebuilt to J50.
Don. 4—25/2/33.**G.**
Don. 2/8—19/9/36.**G.**
Don. 4/11—2/12/39.**G.**
Don. 16/1—6/2/43.**G.**
Don. 25/11—9/12/44.**G.**
Don. 4/12/45—3/1/46.**G.**
Don. 13/3—7/4/49.**G.**
Don. 22—23/8/50.**N/C.**
Don. 7/11—7/12/51.**G.**
Don. 4/11—2/12/54.**G.**
Don. 30/7—30/8/58.**G.**

BOILERS:
6778 *(exR1 137).*
7385 *(exJ55 3790)* 24/8/29.
8768 *(new)* 19/9/36.
8676 *(ex3220)* 2/12/39.
9509 *(new)* 3/1/46.
21847 *(reno from 8486)* 7/12/51.
21827 *(ex68933)* 2/12/54.
21913 *(exC12 67365)* 30/8/58.

SHEDS:
Bradford.
Low Moor 12/1/58.
Stockton 4/5/58.
Selby 14/6/39.
Copley Hill 13/9/59.
Ardsley 27/9/59.
Copley Hill 12/6/60.

RENUMBERED:
3159 5/12/25.
3182 16/6/45.
8892 17/11/46.
68892 7/4/49.

CONDEMNED: 23/9/63.
Into Dar. for cut up 10/63.

3160

Doncaster 1420.

To traffic 2/1914.

REPAIRS:
Don. 11/12/22—24/3/23.**G.**
Don. 19/6—20/9/24.**G.**
Don. 14/7—29/8/28.**G.**
Don. 7—28/11/31.**G.**
Rebuilt to J50.
Don. 22/12/34—19/1/35.**G.**
Don. 27/11—11/12/37.**G.**
Don. 5/10—2/11/40.**G.**
Don. 17/6—24/7/42.**G.**
Cow. 4/5—14/6/44.**G.**
Sent to Stranraer engine shed 29/6/45 for return to LNER.
Don. 15/8—7/9/46.**G.**
Don. 26/2—29/3/47.**G.**
Don. 26/9—19/10/50.**G.**
Don. 8/4—5/5/54.**G.**
Don. 16/10—21/11/57.**G.**
Don. 29/9/59. *Not Repaired.*

BOILERS:
6797 *(ex R1 156).*
6791 *(ex161)* 20/9/24.
6779 *(ex3212)* 29/8/28.
7966 *(ex1081)* 28/11/31.
21805 *(re. fm. 10578)* 19/10/50.
21948 *(reno from 10573)* 5/5/54.
21879 *(ex68911)* 21/11/57.

SHEDS:
Ardsley.
Immingham 29/10/28.
Ardsley 23/2/29.
Doncaster 16/1/42.
WD 17/6/42.
Doncaster 29/6/45.
Immingham 12/8/45.
Frodingham 17/7/46.
Doncaster 24/9/46.
Immingham 18/5/52.
Stratford 6/3/55.
Colwick 29/1/56.

RENUMBERED:
3160 20/9/24.
3183 18/5/45. *By LNER rep.*
8893 29/9/46.
68893 19/10/50.

CONDEMNED: 5/10/59.
Cut up at Doncaster.

3161

Doncaster 1419.

To traffic 2/1914.

REPAIRS:
Don. 28/2—9/6/21.**G.**
Don. 27/10/24—24/1/25.**G.**
Don. 31/5—11/8/28.**G.**

A further ten engines, Nos.211 to 220, and the same as the No.168 series, were built at Doncaster from June to September 1919. Like the previous twenty they had grey livery with white letters and numbers shaded with black. On this batch the forward sanding gear operated on the driving wheels instead of the leading pair (*see* previous illustration), to which arrangement the earlier engines were soon altered.

The boilers on all thirty engines had been used previously on R1 class, and then had the barrel shortened. Two of these were in three rings instead of the normal two and were used on Nos.(3)174 from April 1915 to October 1928 and 3178 from February 1924 to March 1934. They had originally been ordered for use on Stirling single wheelers and had tall domes. All the boilers used on J51 class had Ramsbottom safety valves.

No.215 was the first ex works after Grouping. Out 10th January 1923, it was still in grey with number on the bunker but without any initials on the tanks.

Black, presumably with single red lining, and with number on tank in 12in. shaded transfers, then became standard. The first five to get it, all in 1923, had the ampersand in the company initials and were Nos.220 (2nd March), 160 (24th March), 169 (31st March), 157 (3rd May), 216 (13th June). No.170 (10th July) just had LNER whilst No.173ᴺ (22nd September) and 167ᴺ (27th October) got the area suffix. No.169 got the short wide chimney, intended for J50 No.221.

3161 cont./
Don. 6/8—3/9/32.**G.**
Rebuilt to J50.
Don. 7—21/3/36.**G.**
Don. 6—20/7/40.**G.**
Don. 13/2—13/3/43.**G.**
Don. 5/6—13/7/46.**G.**
Don. 25/3—25/4/49.**G.**
Don. 17/3—16/4/52.**G.**
Don. 26/6—10/8/56.**G.**
Str. 4—29/4/60.**C/L.**
Don. 22/9/61. *Not Repaired.*

BOILERS:
6791 *(exR1 150).*
6793 *(exR1 152)* 9/6/21.
8553 *(new)* 3/9/32.
8555 *(ex3218)* 13/3/43.
10520 *(new)* 25/4/49.
21863 *(reno from 8481)* 16/4/52.
21921 *(ex68904)* 10/8/56.

SHEDS:
Ardsley.
Woodford Halse 11/12/40.
Colwick 25/9/42.
Woodford Halse 13/12/42.
Colwick 19/6/49.
Hornsey 28/9/52.
King's Cross 9/7/61.

RENUMBERED:
3161 24/1/25.
3184 23/6/45.
8894 2/6/46.
68894 25/4/49.

CONDEMNED: 22/9/61.
Cut up at Doncaster.

3162

Doncaster 1421.

To traffic 2/1914.

REPAIRS:
Don. 21/9—13/11/20.**G.**
Don. 13/8—7/11/25.**G.**
Don. 28/12/28—26/1/29.**G.**
Don. 13/2—12/3/32.**G.**
Rebuilt to J50.
Don. 13—27/4/35.**G.**
Don. 18—25/1/36.**L.**
Don. 24/9—8/10/38.**G.**
Don. 26/7—16/8/41.**G.**
Don. 10/6—8/7/44.**G.**
Don. 27/10—19/11/47.**G.**
Don. 17/3—28/4/50.**G.**
Don. 28/11—19/12/51.**C/L.**

Don. 21/4—20/5/54.**G.**
Don. 21/5—15/6/57.**G.**
Don. 16/3/60. *Not Repaired.*

BOILERS:
6794 *(exR1 153).*
6790 *(ex178)* 26/1/29.
8142 *(exJ55 3782)* 12/3/32.
8674 *(ex3222)* 8/10/38.
8487 *(exJ4 4107)* 16/8/41.
8686 *(exC12 7383)* 28/4/50.
21949 *(reno from 8312)* 20/5/54.
21918 *(ex68931)* 15/6/57.

SHEDS:
Bradford.
Ardsley 23/3/31.
Bradford 4/4/42.
Ardsley 15/9/57.
Bradford 6/10/57.
Low Moor 12/1/58.

RENUMBERED:
3162 7/11/25.
3185 16/6/45.
8895 17/11/46.
68895 28/4/50.

CONDEMNED: 28/3/60.
Cut up at Doncaster.

3163

Doncaster 1422.

To traffic 3/1914.

REPAIRS:
Don. 31/5—17/7/20.**G.**
Don. 5/7—25/10/24.**G.**
Don. 22/10/27—7/1/28.**G.**
Don. 18/7—8/8/31.**G.**
Don. 12/5—2/6/34.**G.**
Rebuilt to J50.
Don. 8—15/10/38.**G.**
Don. 27/6—18/7/42.**G.**
Don. 8—29/9/45.**G.**
Don. 7/11—13/12/48.**G.**
Don. 15/3—10/4/52.**G.**
Don. 7/7—5/8/55.**G.**
Don. 24/7—21/8/58.**G.**
Don. 23/8/61. *Not Repaired.*

BOILERS:
1614 *(exR1 118).*
6761 *(exR1 130)* 25/10/24.
8677 *(new)* 2/6/34.
9103 *(ex spare & 606)* 29/9/45.
21862 *(reno from 9825)* 10/4/52.
21848 *(ex68934)* 5/8/55.

21828 *(ex68900)* 21/8/58.

SHEDS:
Ardsley.
Annesley 7/12/52.
New England 14/12/58.
Hornsey 24/1/60.
King's Cross 9/7/61.

RENUMBERED:
3163 25/10/24.
3186 23/6/45.
8896 1/12/46.
68896 11/12/48.

CONDEMNED: 23/8/61.
Cut up at Doncaster.

3164

Doncaster 1424.

To traffic 3/1914.

REPAIRS:
Don. 25/4—20/8/21.**G.**
Don. 11/10/24—27/1/25.**G.**
Don. 7/6—14/7/28.**G.**
Don. 9—30/4/32.**G.**
Rebuilt to J50.
Don. 7—21/3/36.**G.**
Don. 19/8—16/9/39.**G.**
Don. 1—15/6/40.**L.**
Don. 13—27/2/43.**G.**
Don. 9/4—11/5/46.**H.**
Don. 11—17/6/46.**L.**
Don. 17/12/47—8/1/48.**L.**
Don. 29/8—7/10/49.**G.**
Don. 16—19/9/52.**N/C.**
Don. 23/7—20/8/53.**G.**
Don. 5/6—14/7/56.**G.**
Don. 5/11/60. *Not Repaired.*

BOILERS:
6787 *(exR1 146).*
6767 *(exR1 136)* 27/1/25.
8551 *(new)* 30/4/32.
8678 *(ex8941)* 7/10/49.
21899 *(reno from 8515)* 20/8/53.

SHEDS:
Bradford.
Low Moor 12/1/58.
Darlington 9/2/58.
Wakefield 14/6/59.
Ardsley 30/10/60.

RENUMBERED:
3164 27/1/25.
3187 16/6/45.

8897 24/11/46.
68897 7/10/49.

CONDEMNED: 5/11/60.
Cut up at Doncaster.

3166

Doncaster 1423.

To traffic 3/1914.

REPAIRS:
Don. 24/11/20—16/4/21.**G.**
Don. 12/10—31/12/25.**G.**
Don. 25/3—7/5/27.**G.**
Don. 26/10—16/11/29.**G.**
Rebuilt to J50.
Don. 13/5—3/6/33.**G.**
Don. 5—19/12/36.**G.**
Don. 16/3—6/4/40.**G.**
Don. 18/4—2/5/42.**G.**
Don. 18/9—8/10/45.**H.**
Don. 1/12/47—9/1/48.**G.**
Don. 15/2—9/3/51.**G.**
Don. 15/3—7/4/54.**G.**
Don. 7/3—6/4/57.**G.**
Don. 10—14/1/58.**N/C.**
Don. 30/12/59. *Not Repaired.*

BOILERS:
1617 *(exR1 124).*
8312 *(new)* 16/11/29.
8483 *(ex8933)* 9/1/48.
21907 *(new)* 9/3/51.
21910 *(ex68976)* 7/4/54.
21950 *(ex68973)* 6/4/57.

SHEDS:
Bradford.
Ardsley 15/9/57.
Darlington 18/5/58.
Wakefield 14/6/59.

RENUMBERED:
3166 31/12/25.
3188 16/6/45.
8898 24/11/46.
68898 9/3/51.

CONDEMNED: 4/1/60.
Cut up at Doncaster.

WORKS CODES:- Cow - Cowlairs. Dar - Darlington. Don - Doncaster. Ghd - Gateshead. Gor - Gorton. Inv - Inverurie. Kit - Kittybrewster. RSH - Robert, Stephenson & Hawthorn. Str - Stratford. Yk - York.
REPAIR CODES:- **C/H** - Casual Heavy. **C/L** - Casual Light. **G** - General. **H-** Heavy. **H/I** - Heavy Intermediate. **L** - Light. **L/I** - Light Intermediate. **N/C** - Non-Classified.

122

The other twenty-two went direct to LNER and their 1924 numbering. Most of the class had low domes and covers to them, a relic of use on Class R1 for working on the Metropolitan Widened Lines, but some ran with taller domes. Bradford Bowling, 1937.

After June 1928 only plain black was used, No.3160 being so when ex works on 29th August 1928. Ardsley 3rd May 1931.

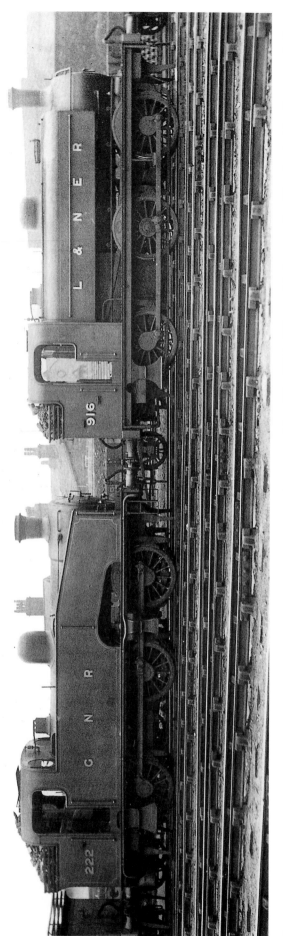

(*above*) Nos.222 to 230 were fitted unusually with a short wide chimney, and all ten engines were - and retained - right hand drive.

(*left*) On 6th September 1931 No.3224 still had the short wide chimney but by the early 1930's these had been replaced by the more usual type. Immingham, 6th September 1931.

(*below*) Only the first of the batch had the customary chimney from building, and to which the other nine changed later.

3167

Doncaster 1427.

To traffic 4/1914.

REPAIRS:
Don. 18/3—8/5/20.**G.**
Don. 25/6—27/10/23.**G.**
Don. 3/4—25/6/27.**G.**
Don. 6/9—11/10/30.**G.**
Rebuilt to J50.
Don. 16/2—2/3/35.**G.**
Don. 1—22/4/39.**G.**
Don. 14—28/11/42.**G.**
Don. 23/7—23/8/45.**H.**
Don. 5—28/11/47.**G.**
Don. 15—25/6/48.**L.**
Don. 8/3—5/4/51.**G.**
Str. 20/10—2/12/53.**G.**
Don. 31/7—30/8/57.**G.**
Don. 3—5/9/57.**N/C.**

BOILERS:
6796 *(exR1 155) (sup.).*
8446 *(new) (sat.)* 11/10/30.
8489 *(ex3170)* 22/4/39.
21906 *(new)* 5/4/51.
21961 *(reno from 8689)* 2/12/53.
21806 *(ex68976)* 30/8/57.

SHEDS:
Ardsley.
Doncaster 6/2/40.
Norwich 1/5/49.
Stratford 3/4/60.

RENUMBERED:
167ɴ 27/10/23.
3167 25/6/27.
3189 26/5/45.
8899 29/11/46.
68899 25/6/48.

CONDEMNED: 4/12/60. *At Stratford.*

3168

Doncaster 1456.

To traffic 12/1914.

REPAIRS:
Don. 25/10/20—9/4/21.**G.**
Don. 15/8—15/11/24.**G.**
Don. 25/5—3/8/28.**G.**
Don. 26/12/31—23/1/32.**G.**
Rebuilt to J50.
Don. 6—13/4/35.**G.**
Don. 10—24/12/38.**G.**
Don. 14/2—7/3/42.**G.**
Don. 3/2—3/3/45.**G.**
Don. 30/10—28/11/47.**G.**

Don. 12/5—5/6/51.**G.**
Don. 22/9—20/10/54.**G.**
Don. 30/6—31/7/58.**G.**
Don. 11/1/62. *Not Repaired.*

BOILERS:
1618 *(ex R1 121).*
8513 *(new)* 23/1/32.
8142 *(ex3162)* 24/12/38.
8444 *(ex3176)* 7/3/42.
8449 *(ex3240)* 3/3/45.
21914 *(new)* 5/6/51.
21828 *(ex68944)* 20/10/54.
21909 *(exC12 67357)* 31/7/58.

SHED:
Ardsley.

RENUMBERED:
3168 15/11/24.
8900 19/5/46.
68900 5/6/51.

CONDEMNED: 22/1/62.
Cut up at Doncaster.

3169

Doncaster 1457.

To traffic 12/1914.

REPAIRS:
Don. 5/7—18/9/20.**G.**
Don. 1/1—31/3/23.**G.**
Don. 27/3—26/6/26.**G.**
Don. 31/12/29—1/2/30.**G.**
Rebuilt to J50.
Don. 2—23/12/33.**G.**
Don. 12/6—3/7/37.**G.**
Don. 30/11—21/12/40.**G.**
Don. 23/10—20/11/43.**G.**
Don. 10—31/8/46.**G.**
Don. 6—30/12/49.**G.**
Don. 13—21/11/50.**N/C.**
Don. 4—27/3/53.**G.**
Don. 10—12/10/55.**C/L.**
Don. 19—24/9/56.**C/L.**
Don. 9—14/11/56.**C/L.**
Don. 3—31/1/57.**G.**
Don. 19—23/10/57.**N/C.**
Don. 8/10/60. *Not Repaired.*

BOILERS:
6764 *(exR1 129).*
1619 *(ex171)* 26/6/26.
8325 *(new)* 1/2/30.
8304 *(ex3176)* 3/7/37.
8144 *(exC12 4535)* 21/12/40.
9641 *(new)* 31/8/46.
8509 *(ex8929)* 30/12/49.
21891 *(reno from 9641)* 27/3/53.
21922 *(ex68969)* 31/1/57.

SHED:
Ardsley.

RENUMBERED:
3169 26/6/26.
8901 19/5/46.
68901 30/12/49.

CONDEMNED: 8/10/60.
Cut up at Doncaster.

3170

Doncaster 1458.

To traffic 12/1914.

REPAIRS:
Don. 21/6—21/8/20.**G.**
Don. 5/3—10/7/23.**G.**
Don. 20/2—5/5/28.**G.**
Don. 7—28/3/31.**G.**
Rebuilt to J50.
Don. 18/5—8/6/35.**G.**
Don. 24/9—1/10/38.**G.**
Don. 23/1—13/2/43.**G.**
Don. 10/6—12/7/47.**G.**
Don. 9—27/10/50.**L/I.**
Don. 18/3—15/6/53.**G.**
Don. 14—30/3/57.**G.**
Don. 30/9/60. *Not Repaired.*

BOILERS:
6780 *(exR1 139).*
8489 *(new)* 28/3/31.
8552 *(ex3174)* 1/10/38.
9101 *(ex8980)* 12/7/47.
9101 reno.21808 27/10/50.
21803 *(ex68913)* 15/6/53.
21938 *(new)* 30/3/57.

SHEDS:
Bradford.
Ardsley 22/2/53.

RENUMBERED:
3170 at shed 2/25.
8902 21/7/46.
68902 27/10/50.

CONDEMNED: 30/9/60.
Cut up at Doncaster.

3171

Doncaster 1459.

To traffic 2/1915.

REPAIRS:
Don. 25/10/20—31/3/21.**G.**
Don. 18/8—29/11/24.**G.**
Don. 5/11—28/12/28.**G.**

Don. 26/3—16/4/32.**G.**
Rebuilt to J50.
Don. 25/5—8/6/35.**G.**
Don. 18/2—4/3/39.**G.**
Don. 15—29/8/42.**G.**
Don. 1—29/12/45.**G.**
Don. 14/2—5/3/49.**G.**
Don. 19—22/9/50.**N/C.**
Don. 22/11—19/12/51.**G.**
Don. 27/12/51—14/1/52.**C/L.**
Don. 12/4—19/5/56.**G.**
Don. 14/4/61. *Not Repaired.*

BOILERS:
1619 *(exR1 125).*
6781 *(exR1 141)* 29/11/24.
8550 *(new)* 16/4/32.
8670 *(ex3178)* 29/8/42.
9507 *(new)* 29/12/45.
21849 *(reno fm. 9826)* 19/12/51.

SHEDS:
Ardsley.
Hornsey 19/10/52.

RENUMBERED:
3171 29/11/24.
8903 19/5/46.
68903 5/3/49.

CONDEMNED: 14/4/61.
Cut up at Doncaster.

3172

Doncaster 1460.

To traffic 3/1915.

REPAIRS:
Don. 21/5—27/7/20.**G.**
Don. 30/10/24—14/2/25.**G.**
Don. 1/9—3/11/28.**G.**
Don. 22/2—15/3/30.**G.**
Rebuilt to J50.
Don. 3—17/3/34.**G.**
Don. 12/6—10/7/37.**G.**
Don. 12/10—9/11/40.**G.**
Don. 3—17/4/43.**G.**
Don. 24/8—21/9/46.**G.**
Don. 13/12/49—13/1/50.**G.**
Don. 23—30/10/51.**N/C.**
Don. 20/1—12/2/53.**G.**
Don. 3/7—4/8/56.**G.**
Don. 17—24/4/57.**N/C.**
Don. 24/7—26/8/59.**G.**

BOILERS:
6765 *(exR1 134).*
6787 *(ex164)* 14/2/25.
7383 *(exJ57 3140A)* 15/3/30.
8063 *(ex3173)* 9/11/40.
9643 *(new)* 21/9/46.
9641 *(ex8901)* 13/1/50.

Ex works 26th April 1926, No.3222 had its LNER lettering and number, note the two lamp irons at the front right hand corner were still fitted although their purpose was no longer needed. Colwick.

No.3227, ex works 22nd November 1930, had lost the redundant lamp iron, but still had a short wide chimney which it kept until it went to works on 18th March 1933. Note load class 4 collar on the vacuum brake standpipe.

No.3222 at Ardsley after its 30th July 1938 shopping because it has CLASS J50 painted on the buffer beam, this being introduced in March 1938. The chimney has been changed, the redundant lamp iron taken off, and plating has been fitted inside the coal bunker rails (compare with the illustration of No.3222 at the top of page 127). Ardsley shed.

Between 9th February and 28th June 1924, ten more J50 class, Nos.3231 to 3240 were built at Doncaster. They had LNER lettering and numbering and normal style chimney, but were fitted - un-necessarily - with the two lamp irons at the front right hand corner. On the bunker they had half-round rails instead of the flat bar used for the previous ten.

3172 cont./
21921 *(new)* 12/2/53.
21881 *(ex68967)* 4/8/56.
21920 *(ex68965)* 26/8/59.

SHEDS:
Copley Hill.
Ardsley 4/2/29.
Wakefield 22/2/59.

RENUMBERED:
3172 14/2/25.
8904 19/5/46.
68904 13/1/50.

CONDEMNED: 23/9/63.
Cut up at Darlington 10/63.

_____

3173

Doncaster 1461.

To traffic 3/1915.

REPAIRS:
Don. 23/3—18/6/21.**G.**
Don. 23/5—22/9/23.**G.**
Don. 27/10/26—22/1/27.**G.**
Don. 1—29/3/30.**G.**
Rebuilt to J50.
Don. 24/3—14/4/34.**G.**
Don. 22/1—5/2/38.**G.**
Don. 5/10—2/11/40.**G.**
Don. 17/4—1/5/43.**L.**
Don. 18/9—2/10/43.**G.**
Don. 5—19/5/45.**L.**
Don. 4—25/5/46.**H.**
Don. 24/4—20/5/49.**G.**
Don. 23/3—24/4/52.**G.**
Don. 12/1—7/2/55.**G.**
Don. 30/5—14/7/58.**G.**

BOILERS:
6784 *(exR1 143).*
7386 *(exJ57 3685)* 29/3/30.
8063 *(exJ55 3918)* 5/2/38.
8303 *(ex3217)* 2/11/40.
8443 *(ex3212)* 2/10/43.
7965 *(ex1079)* 25/5/46.
10519 *(new)* 20/5/49.
10519 reno.21864 24/4/52.
21831 *(ex68978)* 7/2/55.
21860 *(ex68910)* 14/7/58.

SHEDS:
Ardsley.
Copley Hill 8/9/33.
Ardsley 9/11/33.
Doncaster 24/5/37.
Stratford 1/6/46.
Norwich 1/1/49.
Stratford 3/4/60.

RENUMBERED:
173ɴ 22/9/23.
3173 22/1/27.
8905 14/4/46.
68905 20/5/49.

CONDEMNED: 4/12/60. *At Stratford..*

_____

3174

Doncaster 1462.

To traffic 4/1915.

REPAIRS:
Don. 23/3—14/7/21.**G.**
Don. 3/9—29/11/24.**G.**
Don. 8/10—28/11/28.**G.**
Don. 23/4—14/5/32.**G.**
Rebuilt to J50.
Don. 28/9—12/10/35.**G.**
Don. 14—21/5/38.**G.**
Don. 30/8—27/9/41.**G.**
Don. 18/11—2/12/44.**G.**
Don. 24—31/3/45.**L.**
Don. 28/2—14/4/48.**G.**
Don. 26/2—20/3/51.**G.**
Str. 12/6—21/7/53.**N/C.**
Don. 1—31/1/55.**G.**
Don. 6/5/59. *Not Repaired.*

BOILERS:
1388 *(exR1 116).*
1613 *(ex3214)* 28/11/28.
8552 *(new)* 14/5/32.
8311 *(ex3157)* 21/5/38.
21818 *(reno from 8448)* 20/3/51.
21903 *(exC12 67367)* 31/1/55.

SHEDS:
Bradford.
Hornsey 22/2/53.

RENUMBERED:
3174 29/11/24.
8906 28/7/46.
68906 10/4/48.

CONDEMNED: 6/5/59.
Cut up at Doncaster.

_____

3175

Doncaster 1463.

To traffic 5/1915.

REPAIRS:
Don. 19/7—13/10/20.**G.**
Don. 14/10/24—17/1/25.**G.**
Don. 31/1—14/4/27.**G.**
Don. 26/7—16/8/30.**G.**

Don. 1—22/10/32.**G.**
Rebuilt to J50.
Don. 24/10—7/11/36.**G.**
Don. 28/9—19/10/40.**G.**
Don. 24/7—4/9/43.**G.**
Don. 29/9—13/10/45.**G.**
Don. 30/1—22/2/49.**G.**
Don. 13/3—3/4/52.**G.**
Don. 19/5—16/6/56.**G.**
Don. 22/11—10/12/60.**C/L.**
Don. 26/4/61. *Not Repaired.*

BOILERS:
6782 *(exR1 141).*
872 *(exR1 117)* 17/1/25.
8556 *(new)* 22/10/32.
8154 *(ex3226)* 19/10/40.
8485 *(ex583)* 13/10/45.
21861 *(reno from 8266)* 3/4/52.

SHEDS:
Ardsley.
Hornsey 22/2/53.

RENUMBERED:
3175 17/1/25.
8907 26/5/46.
68907 22/2/49.

CONDEMNED: 26/4/61.
Cut up at Doncaster.

_____

3176

Doncaster 1464.

To traffic 6/1915.

REPAIRS:
Don. 15/5—4/11/22.**G.**
Don. 29/1—24/4/26.**G.**
Don. 24/8—21/9/29.**G.**
Rebuilt to J50.
Don. 22/7—5/8/33.**G.**
Don. 10—17/4/37.**G.**
Don. 16—21/5/38.**G.**
Don. 20/8—21/9/41.**G.**
Don. 19/8—2/9/44.**G.**
Don. 3/9—17/10/47.**G.**
Don. 23/10—17/11/50.**G.**
Don. 8/6—14/7/53.**G.**
Don. 4—10/11/54.**C/L.**
Don. 9/5—9/6/56.**G.**
Don. 10/6—23/7/60.**G.**

BOILERS:
1620 *(exR1 121).*
8304 *(new)* 21/9/29.
7923 *(ex583)* 17/4/37.
8444 *(ex3213)* 21/5/38.
9250 *(new)* 21/9/41.
21809 *(reno fm. 8151)* 17/11/50.
21810 *(ex68925)* 14/7/53.
21937 *(ex68973)* 23/7/60.

SHEDS:
Ardsley.
Copley Hill 11/4/43.
Doncaster 22/12/43.
Bradford 23/9/45.
Low Moor 12/1/58.
Middlesbrough 4/5/58.
Thornaby 1/6/58.
Low Moor 25/1/59.
Wakefield 23/12/62.

RENUMBERED:
3176 24/4/26.
8908 28/7/46.
69808 17/11/50.

CONDEMNED: 23/9/63.
Cut up at Darlington 10/63.

_____

3178

Doncaster 1465.

To traffic 6/1915.

REPAIRS:
Don. 30/3—22/5/20.**G.**
Don. 1/12/23—23/2/24.**G.**
Don. 15/10—24/12/27.**G.**
Don. 15/11—6/12/30.**G.**
Don. 17/3—14/4/34.**G.**
Rebuilt to J50.
Don. 12/6—3/7/37.**G.**
Don. 2—23/8/41.**G.**
Don. 1—22/4/44.**G.**
Don. 11/5—8/6/46.**G.**
Don. 1—23/1/48.**H.**
Don. 3—26/8/49.**G.**
Don. 14—17/4/51.**N/C.**
Don. 5/6—11/7/52.**G.**
Don. 8/8—2/9/55.**G.**
Don. 5—8/11/56.**N/C.**
Don. 28/3/60. *Not Repaired.*

BOILERS:
6790 *(exR1 149).*
1391 *(exR1 128)* 23/2/24.
8670 *(new)* 14/4/34.
9249 *(new)* 23/8/41.
8512 *(ex8923)* 26/8/49.
21873 *(reno from 8764)* 11/7/52.
21886 *(exC12 67387)* 2/9/55.

SHEDS:
Ardsley.
Hatfield 16/9/38.
Ardsley 22/11/38.
Darlington 18/5/58.
Stockton 25/5/58.
Darlington 14/9/58.
Wakefield 14/6/59.

Between 24th August 1929 (3159) and 30th March 1935 (3158), ten engines, Nos.3157 to 3164, 3166 and 3167 which were built in 1914 with 4ft 2in. diameter boilers, were rebuilt with a 4ft 5in. boiler and transferred from J51 class to J50 class.

These ten engines had only a short bunker on which a cage was mounted to increase the coal holding capacity. In December 1939 when class parts were introduced, these ten became J50 Part 1.

The ten class J51, Nos.3168 to 3176 and 3178 built December 1914 to June 1915, had their boilers changed from 4ft 2in. to 4ft 5in. diameter between 21st September 1929 (3176) and 14th April 1934 (3178) to become J50 class, and in December 1939 were made Part 2 because of their bigger bunkers and heavier weight. Note the retention of the shorter front end of the side tanks.

Ten similar J51 engines, Nos.3211 to 3220 built June to September 1919, got 4ft 5in. boilers to become Class J50 between 16th March 1929 (3211) and 15th October 1932 (3218) and Part 2 in 1939. Those that got new boilers had Ross 'pops'.

3178 cont./
RENUMBERED:
  3178 23/2/24.
  8909 18/8/46.
  E8909 23/1/48.
  68909 26/8/49.

CONDEMNED: 4/4/60.
Cut up at Doncaster.

_____

3211

Doncaster 1492.

To traffic 6/1919.

REPAIRS:
Don. 21/11/21—11/3/22.**G.**
Don. 13/10/25—2/1/26.**G.**
Don. 16/2—16/3/29.**G.**
Rebuilt to J50.
Don. 24/2—28/5/32.**G.**
Don. 22/2—7/3/36.**G.**
Don. 13/1—10/2/40.**G.**
Don. 29/6—6/7/40.**L.**
Don. 5—19/9/42.**G.**
Don. 3/11—1/12/45.**G.**
Don. 28/9—12/10/46.**L.**
Don. 1—11/1/47.**G.**
Don. 9—25/3/49.**G.**
Don. 15/2/51.**N/C.**
Don. 6/3—13/4/51.**G.**
Don. 29/9—27/10/54.**G.**
Don. 17/5—18/6/58.**G.**

BOILERS:
  1621 *(ex158).*
  8156 *(new)* 16/3/29.
  8447 *(ex3227)* 7/3/36.
  8268 *(ex2792)* 19/9/42.
  10517 *(new)* 25/3/49.
  21820 *(reno from 9818)* 13/4/51.
  21860 *(exC12 67384)* 27/10/54.
  21944 *(exC12 67362)* 18/6/58.

SHEDS:
Ardsley.
Wakefield 22/2/59.

RENUMBERED:
  3211 2/1/26.
  8910 26/5/46.
  68910 25/3/49.

CONDEMNED: 26/11/62.
Into Don. for cut up 19/12/62.

_____

3212

Doncaster 1493.

To traffic 7/1919.

REPAIRS:
Don. 20/10/22—3/2/23.**G.**
Don. 27/3—3/7/26.**G.**
Don. 26/7—30/8/30.**G.**
Rebuilt to J50.
Don. 24/3—14/4/34.**G.**
Don. 14—28/8/37.**G.**
Don. 19/10—16/11/40.**G.**
Don. 14—28/8/43.**G.**
Don. 4/1—1/2/47.**G.**
Don. 25/12/49—26/1/50.**G.**
Don. 15/8—19/9/52.**G.**
Don. 7—24/12/55.**C/L.**
Don. 18/9—12/10/57.**G.**
Don. 22/11/60. *Not Repaired.*
To Service Stock 15/2/61.

BOILERS:
  6779 *(exR1 138).*
  6782 *(ex175)* 3/7/26.
  8443 *(new)* 30/8/30.
  8689 *(ex3238)* 28/8/43.
  8302 *(exC12 7361)* 26/1/50.
  21879 *(reno fm. 10520)* 19/9/52.
  21874 *(ex68891)* 12/10/57.
  21874 reno. S.B.1175 15/2/61.

SHEDS:
Ardsley.
Copley Hill 23/4/29.
Ardsley 2/6/37.
Copley Hill 27/9/37.
Doncaster Works 15/2/61.

RENUMBERED:
  3212 3/7/26.
  8911 1/6/46.
  68911 26/1/50.
  DEPT'L No.10 15/2/61.

WITHDRAWN: 22/11/60.
CONDEMNED: 30/5/65.
*Sold for scrap to T.W. Ward,
Beighton, 7/65.*

_____

3213

Doncaster 1494.

To traffic 7/1919.

REPAIRS:
Don. 11/12/22—2/3/23.**G.**
Don. 7/4—10/7/26.**G.**
Don. 26/7—23/8/30.**G.**
Rebuilt to J50.
Don. 24/11—8/12/34.**G.**
Don. 5—12/3/38.**G.**
Don. 26/4—24/5/41.**G.**
Don. 29/7—19/8/44.**G.**
Don. 20/7—31/8/47.**G.**
Don. 26/12/48—14/1/49.**C/L.**
Don. 2—27/10/50.**G.**
Don. 11/8—4/9/53.**G.**
Don. 30/4—2/6/56.**G.**

BOILERS:
  1616 *(exR1 120).*
  8444 *(new)* 23/8/30.
  8305 *(exC12 4515)* 12/3/38.
  8768 *(ex3226)* 19/8/44.
  8548 *(exC12 7365)* 31/8/47.
  21807 *(rn. fm. 10579)* 27/10/50.
  21941 *(reno from 8763)* 4/9/53.

SHEDS:
Ardsley.
Copley Hill 19/2/32.
Ardsley 4/10/32.
Copley Hill 1/12/32.
Ardsley 16/11/34.
Woodford Halse 20/2/35.
Leicester 6/4/38.
Ardsley 29/8/43.
Bradford 19/3/44.
Low Moor 12/1/58.
Hull Dairycoates 9/2/58.
Goole 11/5/58.
Low Moor 25/1/59.

RENUMBERED:
  3213 10/7/26.
  8912 20/1/46.
  68912 14/1/49.

CONDEMNED: 14/9/59.
Into Don. for cut up 17/9/59.

_____

3214

Doncaster 1495.

To traffic 7/1919.

REPAIRS:
Don. 14/2—10/5/23.**G.**
Don. 15/10/26—8/1/27.**G.**
Don. 7/9—12/10/29.**G.**
Rebuilt to J50.
Don. 15—29/7/33.**G.**
Don. 16—23/1/37.**G.**
Don. 17/8—7/9/40.**G.**
Don. 10—24/7/43.**G.**
Don. 13/1—22/2/47.**G.**
Don. 12/9—6/10/50.**G.**
Don. 29/4—22/5/53.**G.**
Don. 16/12/55—20/1/56.**G.**
Don. 17—25/4/59.**C/L.**
Don. 20/8/60. *Not Repaired.*

BOILERS:
  1613 *(exR1 119).*
  6797 *(ex160)* 8/1/27.
  8307 *(new)* 12/10/29.
  8516 *(exC12 4014)* 22/2/47.
  21803 *(reno fm. 10577)* 6/10/50.
  21894 *(reno from 8766)* 22/5/53.

SHED:
Copley Hill.

RENUMBERED:
  3214 8/1/27.
  8913 17/3/46.
  68913 6/10/50.

CONDEMNED: 29/8/60.
Cut up at Doncaster.

_____

3215

Doncaster 1496.

To traffic 7/1919.

REPAIRS:
Don. 31/10/22—10/1/23.**G.**
Don. 9/10—19/12/25.**G.**
Don. 10/12/28—26/1/29.**G.**
Don. 31/1—28/2/31.**G.**
Rebuilt to J50.
Don. 23/2—9/3/35.**G.**
Don. 17/12/38—7/1/39.**G.**
Don. 1—29/8/42.**G.**
Don. 19/5—23/6/45.**G.**
Don. 14/2—12/3/48.**G.**
Don. 4/7—18/8/50.**G.**
Don. 15/6—17/7/53.**G.**
Don. 28—31/3/55.**N/C.**
Don. 1/4—4/5/57.**G.**
Don. 2—20/1/59.**C/H.**
Don. 12/11/60. *Not Repaired.*
To Service Stock 15/2/61.

BOILERS:
  6789 *(exR1 148).*
  1614 *(ex3163)* 26/1/29.
  8486 *(new)* 28/2/31.
  8171 *(ex3231)* 29/8/42.
  8149 *(ex3158)* 23/6/45.
  8487 *(ex8895)* 18/8/50.
  21895 *(reno from 9820)* 17/7/53.
  21910 *(ex68898)* 4/5/57.
  21805 *(ex68937)* 20/1/59.
  21805 reno.S.B.1176 15/2/61.

SHEDS:
Ardsley.
Doncaster Works 15/2/61.

RENUMBERED:
  3215 19/12/25.
  8914 26/5/46.

All except five of the thirty conversions from J51 to J50 got boilers built 1926 or later and these had Ross 'pop' safety valves. The boilers used for Nos.3159, 3172, 3173, 3216 and 3219 had been built in 1917 as replacements on J55 and J57 classes and they had Ramsbottom safety valves.

The LNER adopted this class as the standard goods shunter and from 18th March to 5th August 1926 built twelve more J50 numbered between 583 and 610 for Southern Area sheds. They were similar to those built in 1922 but differed in details and to suit composite loading gauge, had a more rounded cab roof.

3215 cont./
E8914 12/3/48.
68914 18/8/50.
DEPT'L No. 11 15/2/61

WITHDRAWN: 12/11/60.
CONDEMNED: 30/5/65.
*Sold for scrap to T.W. Ward,
Beighton, 7/65.*

_____

3216

Doncaster 1497.

To traffic 7/1919.

REPAIRS:
Don. 12/3—13/6/23.**G**.
Don. 7/6—1/9/26.**G**.
Don. 20/4—11/5/29.**G**.
Rebuilt to J50.
Don. 30/7—27/8/32.**G**.
Don. 22/8—5/9/36.**G**.
Don. 11/5—1/6/40.**G**.
Don. 24/4—8/5/43.**G**.
Don. 14—28/10/44.**G**.
Don. 20/7—5/9/47.**G**.
Don. 23/11—19/12/50.**G**.
Don. 28/7—24/8/53.**G**.
Don. 4—9/2/56.**N/C**.
Don. 5/4—9/5/57.**G**.
Don. 4/10/60. *Not Repaired.*

BOILERS:
6766 *(exR1 122).*
7387 *(exJ55 3636A)* 11/5/29.
8762 *(new)* 5/9/36.
8448 *(ex8922)* 5/9/47.
21812 *(reno fm. 8516)* 19/12/50.
21940 *(reno from 8769)* 24/8/53.
21939 *(new)* 9/5/57.

SHEDS:
Ardsley.
Copley Hill 12/5/30.
Ardsley 2/1/31.

RENUMBERED:
  3216 1/9/26.
  8915 20/1/46.
68915 19/12/50.

CONDEMNED: 4/10/60.
Cut up at Doncaster.

_____

3217

Doncaster 1498.

To traffic 8/1919.

REPAIRS:
Don. 21/11/21—4/3/22.**G**.

Don. 18/8—21/11/25.**G**.
Don. 16/2—23/3/29.**G**.
Rebuilt to J50.
Don. 18/1—15/2/30.**L**.
Don. 6/8—17/9/32.**G**.
Don. 25/7—8/8/36.**G**.
Don. 6—20/7/40.**G**.
Don. 1—29/11/41.**L**.
Don. 22/5—19/6/43.**G**.
Don. 3/11—14/12/46.**H**.
Don. 14—28/1/49.**C/L**.
Don. 17/8—20/9/50.**G**.
Don. 29/6—24/7/53.**G**.
Don. 24—28/3/56.**N/C**.
Don. 5/8—7/9/57.**G**.
Don. 11/3/61. *Not Repaired.*

BOILERS:
6785 *(exR1 144).*
8153 *(new)* 23/3/29.
8303 *(exC12 4019)* 8/8/36.
8446 *(ex3167)* 20/7/40.
8765 *(exC12 4514)* 14/12/46.
21801 *(reno from 8149)* 20/9/50.
21896 *(reno from 9308)* 24/7/53.
21891 *(ex68901)* 7/9/57.

SHED:
Ardsley.

RENUMBERED:
  3217 21/11/25.
  8916 20/1/46.
68916 28/1/49.

CONDEMNED: 10/4/61.
Cut up at Doncaster.

_____

3218

Doncaster 1499.

To traffic 8/1919.

REPAIRS:
Don. 21/8—11/12/22.**G**.
Lettered GNR and grey livery.
Don. 18/8—14/11/25.**G**.
Don. 27/7—17/8/29.**G**.
Don. 24/9—15/10/32.**G**.
Rebuilt to J50.
Don. 11—25/5/35.**G**.
Don. 11—18/2/39.**G**.
Don. 18/4—16/5/42.**G**.
Don. 22/1—5/2/44.**L**.
Don. 6—20/10/45.**G**.
Don. 18/7—17/8/48.**G**.
Don. 28/4—22/5/52.**G**.
Don. 9/7—21/8/56.**G**.
Don. 28/11/60—3/1/61.**G**.
To Service Stock 16/9/62.
Don. 1/2—6/3/63.**L**.

BOILERS:
6760 *(exR1 125).*
8555 *(new)* 15/10/32.
8674 *(ex3162)* 16/5/42.
8672 *(ex8918)* 17/8/48.
21867 *(reno from 9111)* 22/5/52.
21863 *(ex68894)* 21/8/56.
21824 *(ex68971)* 3/1/61.
21824 reno.S.B.4523 16/9/62.

SHEDS:
Ardsley.
Doncaster 28/11/48.
Hornsey 19/10/52.
Doncaster 9/7/61.
Doncaster Works 16/9/62.

RENUMBERED:
  3218 14/11/25.
  8917 26/5/46.
68917 14/8/48.
DEPT'L No. 12 16/9/62.

WITHDRAWN: 16/9/62.
CONDEMNED: 30/5/65.
*Sold for scrap to T.W. Ward,
Beighton, 7/65.*

_____

3219

Doncaster 1500.

To traffic 9/1919.

REPAIRS:
Don. 5/7—19/10/22.**G**.
Don. 23/10/25—2/1/26.**G**.
Don. 26/9—7/11/28.**G**.
Don. 5—26/4/30.**G**.
Rebuilt to J50.
Don. 24/3—7/4/34.**G**.
Don. 30/4—7/5/38.**G**.
Don. 14—28/2/42.**G**.
Dar. 11—14/7/42.**L**.
LMS. 27/8—11/11/43.**L**.
At Stranraer shed.
*Sent to Stranraer engine shed for
return to LNER 29/5/45.*
Don. 5—10/11/45.**L**.
Don. 1—29/12/45.**G**.
Don. 14/6—19/7/48.**G**.
Don. 28/7—28/8/52.**G**.
Str. 22/4—4/6/53.**C/L**.
Don. 17/10—14/11/57.**G**.
Don. 20/7/61. *Not Repaired.*

BOILERS:
6792 *(exR1 151).*
6791 *(ex3160)* 7/11/28.
7384 *(exJ55 3473A)* 26/4/30.
8450 *(ex3228)* 7/5/38.
8672 *(ex3236)* 28/2/42.
9819 *(new)* 19/7/48.
21915 *(new)* 28/8/52.

21951 *(ex68962)* 14/11/57.

SHEDS:
Ardsley.
WD 15/8/42.
Immingham 30/5/45.
Frodingham 11/8/46.
Doncaster 24/9/46.
Hornsey 28/9/52.
King's Cross 9/7/61.

RENUMBERED:
  3219 2/1/26.
  8918 27/1/46.
68918 17/7/48.

CONDEMNED: 20/7/61.
Cut up at Doncaster.

_____

3220

Doncaster 1501.

To traffic 9/1919.

REPAIRS:
Don. 15/11/22—2/3/23.**G**.
Don. 20/4—31/7/26.**G**.
Don. 2—30/11/29.**G**.
Rebuilt to J50.
Don. 12/8—2/9/33.**G**.
Don. 27/7—17/8/35.**G**.
Don. 17/6—8/7/39.**G**.
Don. 20/2—13/3/43.**G**.
Don. 1/6—6/7/46.**G**.
Don. 2—17/8/47.**L**.
Don. 16/10—25/11/49.**G**.
Don. 13—18/8/51.**N/C**.
Don. 1—24/12/52.**G**.
Don. 9/1—3/2/56.**G**.
Don. 5/6—6/7/57.**C/L**.
Don. 21/9/59. *Not Repaired.*

BOILERS:
6786 *(exR1 145).*
8314 *(new)* 30/11/29.
8676 *(new)* 17/8/35.
8513 *(ex3168)* 8/7/39.
8550 *(ex3217)* 13/3/43.
8446 *(ex8990)* 25/11/49.
21920 *(new)* 24/12/52.
21852 *(ex68928)* 3/2/56.

SHED:
Ardsley.

RENUMBERED:
  3220 31/7/26.
  8919 20/1/46.
68919 25/11/49.

CONDEMNED: 21/9/59.
Cut up at Doncaster.

_____

Other differences were balanced wheels, injectors under the footplate, improved ventilator on the cab roof, and raised side tank filler holes. Drive was now on the left hand side and only steam brake was fitted. These twelve had Ross 'pops' and the coupling rods were fluted. From December 1939 they were Part 3.

Seven more, Nos.616, 617, 618, 621, 622, 635 and 636 were built 24th July to 27th October 1926 for the Scottish Area and, when new, only differed by having plain coupling rods. They too became Part 3.

Between 16th November 1926 and 14th May 1927, thirteen more were built for the Southern Area and were numbered between 1037 and 1086. They had one more difference, as Group Standard buffers were introduced on them, these were 2 inches longer, had a square flange and stepped shank.

A final batch of six, Nos.2789 to 2794, built at Doncaster 22nd February to 19th April 1930, also for Southern Area, were similar to the previous thirteen but reverted to fluted coupling rods. In December 1939 these four batches, totalling thirty-eight engines, all became Part 3.

No.2794 was the last J50 built at Doncaster. Ex works in April 1930, note that it had open coal rails. Southern Area were also to have had twenty-two on the 1931, fifteen on the 1935, and six on the 1937 construction programmes but all were cancelled due to trade depression.

From 10th November 1938 to 1st April 1939, Gorton built eight J50 Nos.599, 600, 602, 605, 606, 608, 611 and 615 on which there were other detail alterations. The safety valves had an $8^{3}/_{8}$in. mounting block inserted between their base and the firebox. Coal rails were discarded and a built-up hopper bunker was put on. There was a reversion to vacuum brake, and carriage heating equipment, including a front end connection, was added, which made them suitable for empty coaching stock workings. These differences put them into Part 4 from 1939.

3221

Doncaster 1544.

To Traffic 10/1922.

REPAIRS:
Don. 7/12/25—30/1/26.**G.**
Don. 18/5—15/6/29.**G.**
Don. 22/8—3/10/31.**G.**
Don. 24/3—14/4/34.**G.**
Don. 31/12/36—9/1/37.**G.**
Don. 20/4—18/5/40.**G.**
Don. 3—24/4/43.**G.**
Don. 30/3—27/4/46.**G.**
Don. 10/10—13/11/47.**H.**
Don. 2/1—4/2/50.**G.**
Str. 27/2—27/3/53.**G.**
Don. 21/2—23/3/56.**C/L.**
Don. 28/3—25/5/57.**G.**
Don. 20/7/61. *Not Repaired.*

BOILERS:
7035 *(exJ4 177).*
8671 *(new)* 14/4/34.
8153 *(ex3217)* 9/1/37.
8159 *(exC12 7365)* 13/11/47.
8689 *(ex8911)* 4/2/50.
21962 *(reno from 8549)* 27/3/53.
21895 *(ex68914)* 25/5/57.

SHEDS:
Ardsley.
New England 19/6/26.
Immingham 26/11/29.
Woodford Halse 8/3/35.
Colwick 1/6/38.
Leicester 11/1/39.
Woodford Halse 3/8/43.
Colwick 19/6/49.
Hornsey 28/9/52.
King's Cross 9/7/61.

RENUMBERED:
3221 30/1/26.
8920 25/4/46.
68920 4/2/50.

CONDEMNED: 20/7/61.
Cut up at Doncaster.

___

3222

Doncaster 1545.

To Traffic 11/1922.

REPAIRS:
Don. 15/2—26/4/26.**G.**
Don. 27/10—12/12/28.**G.**
Don. 15/11—13/12/30.**G.**
Don. 10—31/12/32.**G.**
Don. 27/4—4/5/35.**G.**

Don. 16—30/7/38.**G.**
Don. 3—31/1/42.**G.**
Don. 30/9—14/10/44.**G.**
Don. 14/1—1/2/47.**H.**
Don. 3/1—6/2/48.**G.**
Don. 3—27/7/51.**G.**
Don. 30/11—31/12/55.**G.**
Don. 12—16/5/58.**N/C.**
Don. 26/4/61. *Not Repaired*

BOILERS:
6919 *(exD4 400).*
7381 *(exJ4 4034)* 31/12/32.
8674 *(new)* 4/5/35.
7923 *(ex3176)* 30/7/38.
9251 *(exC12 7358)* 6/2/48.
21830 *(reno from 8552)* 27/7/51.
21885 *(ex68942)* 31/12/55.

SHEDS:
Ardsley.
Colwick 18/6/26.
Lincoln 20/3/28.
Immingham 3/12/29.
Ardsley 27/1/36.
Hornsey 19/10/52.

RENUMBERED:
3222 26/4/26.
8921 15/6/46.
E8921 6/2/48.
68921 27/7/51.

CONDEMNED: 26/4/61.
Cut up at Doncaster.

___

3223

Doncaster 1546.

To Traffic 11/1922.

REPAIRS:
Don. 27/10—26/12/25.**G.**
Don. 27/2—26/5/28.**G.**
Don. 6/9—4/10/30.**G.**
Don. 25/10—16/12/33.**G.**
Don. 12/6—3/7/37.**G.**
Don. 7/9—5/10/40.**G.**
Don. 8—29/4/44.**G.**
Don. 27/3—22/5/47.**G.**
Don. 25/9—25/10/50.**G.**
Don. 30/8—1/10/53.**G.**
Don. 9/7—10/8/56.**G.**
Don. 23/11—19/12/59.**G.**

BOILERS:
364 *(exJ4 1128).*
8448 *(new)* 4/10/30.
8151 *(exC12 7361)* 22/5/47.
21806 *(rn. fm. 10575)* 25/10/50.
21807 *(ex68912)* 1/10/53.
21912 *(ex68942)* 19/12/59.

SHEDS:
Ardsley.
Immingham 29/10/26.
Ardsley 14/10/30.
Bradford 29/10/30.
Low Moor 12/1/58.
Wakefield 23/12/62.

RENUMBERED:
3223 26/12/25.
8922 28/7/46.
68922 25/10/50.

CONDEMNED: 23/9/63.
Into Dar. for cut up 10/63.

___

3224

Doncaster 1547.

To Traffic 11/1922.

REPAIRS:
Don. 1/2—31/3/26.**G.**
Don. 20/6—15/8/28.**G.**
Don. 19/12/31—9/1/32.**G.**
Don. 21/9—12/10/35.**G.**
Don. 4—25/2/39.**G.**
Don. 29/3—12/4/41.**L.**
Don. 17—31/10/42.**G.**
Don. 3/11—1/12/45.**G.**
Don. Shed. 15/12/45.**N/C.**
Don. 14/11—24/12/48.**G.**
Don. 14/1—6/2/52.**G.**
Don. 12/11—8/12/54.**G.**
Don. 6/6—16/7/58.**G.**
Don. 13/12/61. *Not Repaired.*

BOILERS:
1649 *(exJ4 1142).*
8512 *(new)* 9/1/32.
8270 *(ex8927)* 24/12/48.
21853 *(reno from 9252)* 6/2/52.
21820 *(ex68910)* 8/12/54.
21831 *(ex68905)* 16/7/58.

SHEDS:
Ardsley.
Immingham 22/10/26.
Ardsley 16/1/32.
Bradford 27/1/36.
Low Moor 12/1/58.

RENUMBERED:
3224 31/3/26.
8923 21/7/46.
68923 24/12/48.

CONDEMNED: 13/12/61.
Cut up at Doncaster.

___

3225

Doncaster 1548.

To Traffic 11/1922.

REPAIRS:
Don. 28/7—23/10/26.**G.**
Don. 12/11/28—5/1/29.**G.**
Don. 31/1—21/2/31.**G.**
Don. 8—29/7/33.**G.**
Don. 1—8/2/36.**G.**
Don. 22/10—5/11/38.**G.**
Don. 5—26/6/43.**G.**
Don. 9/2—2/3/46.**H.**
Don. 14/5—16/6/50.**G.**
Don. 26/3—23/4/53.**G.**
Don. 10/12/55—12/1/56.**G.**
Don. 30/7—4/9/58.**G.**

BOILERS:
6884 *(ex ?).*
7822 *(exC12 4524)* 29/7/33.
9817 *(exC12 67369)* 16/6/50.
21924 *(new)* 23/4/53.

SHEDS:
Ardsley.
Immingham 3/1/27.
Lincoln 10/3/28.
Immingham 21/3/28.
Keadby 21/3/31.
Frodingham 12/6/32.
Hornsey 25/8/39.
King's Cross 25/4/40.
Gorton 26/3/41.
Doncaster 31/5/43.
Stratford 30/3/46.
Norwich 7/12/49.
Stratford 3/4/60.

RENUMBERED:
3225 23/10/26.
8924 2/6/46.
68924 16/6/50.

CONDEMNED: 14/2/61. *At Stratford.*

___

3226

Doncaster 1549.

To Traffic 11/1922.

REPAIRS:
Don. 28/5—27/8/26.**G.**
Don. 27/8—12/10/28.**G.**
Don. 23/1—13/2/32.**G.**
Don. 4—18/1/36.**G.**
Don. 9/12/39—6/1/40.**G.**
Don. 4/10—1/11/41.**G.**
Don. 15/7—5/8/44.**G.**

Six more, exactly similar, Nos.584, 585, 587, 590, 595 and 598 were built at Gorton from 29th April to 26th August 1939 and they too became Part 4. On these fourteen, the hopper bunker caused much smaller rear windows to be fitted to the cab, and they were the first to have welded side tanks.

Because sanding of the rails was thought to cause interference with track circuits, trials with rail washing gear were made. Ex works 28th May 1932, No.3211 was so equipped for both directions of working, but no others were fitted and the date of removal is unknown.

Some changes of detail were made, especially on the earlier engines. By the mid-1930's the short wide chimney had gone, and from 1931, the open coal rails had plating behind them to minimise spillage of small coal. Redundant lamp irons were taken off, and instead of faceplate injectors the under-footplate type was fitted but placed to the rear of the cab footstep.

From February 1937 all the ninety-five English based engines had the $8^{3}/_{8}$,in. mounting inserted between the safety valves and firebox. By then all had Ross 'pop' type valves. Doncaster works.

3226 cont./
Don. 17/9—17/10/47.**G.**
Don. 6—29/11/50.**H/I.**
Don. 21/4—12/5/53.**G.**
Don. 5—7/10/54.**N/C.**
Don. 29/5—5/7/56.**G.**
Don. 13/7—11/8/60.**G.**
Don. 10—18/3/61.**C/L.**
Don. 10—26/7/62.**C/L.**

BOILERS:
1167 *(ex ?).*
8154 *(new)* 12/10/28.
8768 *(ex3159)* 6/1/40.
8553 *(ex3161)* 5/8/44.
8553 reno.21810 29/11/50.
21893 *(reno fm. 10571)* 12/5/53.
21919 *(ex68938)* 11/8/60.

SHEDS:
Ardsley.
Immingham 3/1/27.
Ardsley 12/10/28.
Copley Hill 18/4/48.

RENUMBERED:
3226 27/8/26.
8925 16/6/46.
68925 29/11/50.

CONDEMNED: 18/3/63.
Into Don. for cut up 9/4/63.

_____

3227

Doncaster 1550.

To Traffic 12/1922.

REPAIRS:
Don. 17/11/25—5/2/26.**G.**
Don. 11/6—15/8/28.**G.**
Don. 1—22/11/30.**G.**
Don. 18/3—8/4/33.**G.**
Don. 7—21/12/35.**G.**
Don. 21—28/5/38.**G.**
Don. 6—20/7/40.**G.**
Don. 20/2—13/3/43.**G.**
Don. 28/7—1/9/45.**G.**
Don. 4/12/47—23/1/48.**G.**
Don. 12/2—2/3/51.**G.**
Don. 15/8—16/9/54.**G.**
Don. 29/10—4/12/58.**G.**
Don. 13/2/62. *Not Repaired.*

BOILERS:
1137 *(exJ4 1127).*
8447 *(new)* 22/11/30.
8314 *(ex3220)* 21/12/35.
9818 *(new)* 23/1/48.
21817 *(reno from 9250)* 2/3/51.
21901 *(exC12 67363)* 16/9/54.
21900 *(exC12 67367)* 4/12/58.

SHEDS:
Ardsley.
Immingham 28/2/27.
Frodingham 11/8/46.
Doncaster 26/9/46.
Immingham 18/5/52.
Doncaster 9/10/55.
Hornsey 26/10/58.
Doncaster 9/7/61.

RENUMBERED:
3227 5/2/26.
8926 16/6/46.
E8926 23/1/48.
68926 2/3/51.

CONDEMNED: 13/2/62.
Cut up at Doncaster.

_____

3228

Doncaster 1551.

To Traffic 12/1922.

REPAIRS:
Don. 4/11/25—20/1/26.**G.**
Don. 15/2—21/4/28.**G.**
Don. 16/8—27/9/30.**G.**
Don. 28/1—18/2/33.**G.**
Don. 3—24/8/35.**G.**
Don. 5—12/2/38.**G.**
Don. 30/3—27/4/40.**G.**
Don. 26/12/42—16/1/43.**G.**
Don. 14/7—18/8/45.**G.**
Don. 7/1—3/2/48.**G.**
Don. 3—28/7/50.**G.**
Don. 20/1—25/2/53.**G.**
Don. 28/8—16/9/55.**C/L.**
Don. 17/3—20/4/56.**G.**
Don. 10/2—19/3/59.**G.**
Don. 15/4/61. *Not Repaired.*

BOILERS:
6987 *(ex ?).*
8450 *(new)* 27/9/30.
7821 *(exC12 4549)* 12/2/38.
8270 *(ex1041)* 16/1/43.
8490 *(exC12 7399)* 3/2/48.
10571 *(new)* 28/7/50.
21889 *(reno from 8446)* 25/2/53.
21910 *(ex68914)* 19/3/59.

SHEDS:
Ardsley.
Immingham 24/2/27.
Annesley 13/10/46.
Hornsey 19/10/52.
Annesley 23/11/52.
Colwick 5/2/56.

RENUMBERED:
3228 20/1/26.
8927 16/6/46.
E8927 3/2/48.
68927 28/7/50.

CONDEMNED: 17/4/61.
Cut up at Doncaster.

_____

3229

Doncaster 1552.

To Traffic 12/1922.

REPAIRS:
Don. 25/2—18/5/26.**G.**
Don. 23/7—19/9/28.**G.**
Don. 10—24/1/31.**G.**
Don. 6—27/5/33.**G.**
Don. 18/4—2/5/36.**G.**
Don. 6/5—10/6/39.**G.**
Don. 6/12/41—3/1/42.**G.**
Don. 22/4—10/5/44.**G.**
Don. 19/1—15/2/47.**G.**
Don. 13/2—18/3/49.**G.**
Don. 24/12/51—18/1/52.**G.**
Don. 30/12/55—2/2/56.**G.**
Don. 27/6—30/7/60.**G.**
To Service Stock 16/9/62.

BOILERS:
6960 *(ex ?).*
8482 *(new)* 24/1/31.
8671 *(exJ4 090)* 15/2/47.
8674 *(ex8917)* 18/3/49.
21852 *(reno from 8488)* 18/1/52.
21838 *(ex68929)* 2/2/56.
21918 *(ex68895)* 30/7/60.
21918 reno. S.B.4524 16/9/62.

SHEDS:
Ardsley.
Immingham 28/2/27.
Doncaster 26/10/36.
Sheffield 29/1/40.
Hornsey 19/10/52.
Doncaster 9/7/61.
Doncaster Works 16/9/62.

RENUMBERED:
3229 18/5/26.
8928 14/4/46.
68928 18/3/49.
DEPT'L No.13 16/9/62.

WITHDRAWN: 16/9/62.
CONDEMNED: 30/5/65.
Sold for scrap to T.W. Ward,
Beighton, 7/65.

_____

3230

Doncaster 1553.

To Traffic 12/1922.

REPAIRS:
Don. 8/1—6/3/26.**G.**
Don. 4/5—21/6/28.**G.**
Don. 6/9—11/10/30.**G.**
Don. 15—29/4/33.**G.**
Don. 16—30/5/36.**G.**
Don. 28/1—11/2/39.**G.**
Don. 27/1—9/3/40.**L.**
Don. 24/5—21/6/41.**G.**
Don. 9—30/10/43.**G.**
Don. 23/6—4/8/45.**G.**
Don. 30/11/47—16/1/48.**G.**
Don. 29/3—27/4/49.**C/L.**
Don. 14/10—10/11/49.**C/H.**
Don. 2—28/8/51.**G.**
Str. 27/7—10/9/55.**G.**
Don. 2/5/61. *Not Repaired.*

BOILERS:
7078 *(ex ?).*
8442 *(new)* 11/10/30.
8509 *(exC12 4508)* 4/8/45.
8687 *(ex8942)* 10/11/49.
21838 *(reno from 9823)* 28/8/51.
21826 *(ex68971)* 10/9/55.

SHEDS:
Ardsley.
Immingham 7/3/27.
Annesley 25/8/46.
Hornsey 19/10/52.

RENUMBERED:
3230 6/3/26.
8929 16/6/46.
E8929 16/1/48.
68929 27/4/49.

CONDEMNED: 2/5/61.
Cut up at Doncaster.

_____

On the seven engines based in Scotland and maintained by Cowlairs, only two, Nos.68952 and 8957 had this safety valve mounting change. Eastfield, 6th May 1950.

Not until the LNER batches were built from 1926 onwards did the wheels have balance weights on them. Doncaster.

The fifty engines built to Great Northern Railway design, both J51 and J50, did not have balances wheels nor were they so altered later. Doncaster, 15th April 1951.

The seven built to work in Scotland were only fitted with normal cab footsteps when delivered to Eastfield shed. Eastfield.

3231

Doncaster 1583.

To Traffic 9/2/24.

REPAIRS:
Don. 17/8—19/10/27.**G.**
Don. 1—22/8/31.**G.**
Don. 16/3—6/4/35.**G.**
Don. 10—31/12/38.**G.**
Don. 1—22/8/42.**G.**
Don. 8—22/9/45.**G.**
Don. 10/10—23/11/48.**G.**
Don. 2/8—1/9/51.**G.**
Str. 29/1—15/4/54.**N/C.**
Str. 26/6—30/7/54.**N/C.**
Don. 2/2—8/3/56.**G.**
Don. 2/2/61. *Not Repaired.*

BOILERS:
6810 *(exD4 1075?).*
8515 *(new)* 22/8/31.
8171 *(exC12 4519)* 6/4/35.
8761 *(exC12 4538)* 22/8/42.
9826 *(new)* 23/11/48.
21839 *(reno from 8762)* 1/9/51.
21887 *(exC12 67368)* 8/3/56.

SHEDS:
Ardsley.
Hornsey 19/10/52.

RENUMBERED:
8930 20/1/46.
68930 20/11/48.

CONDEMNED: 6/2/61.
Cut up at Doncaster.

3232

Doncaster 1586.

To Traffic 23/2/24.

REPAIRS:
Don. 22/7—5/10/27.**G.**
Don. 30/5—20/6/31.**G.**
Don. 23—30/3/35.**G.**
Don. 3—10/12/38.**G.**
Don. 12/12/42—2/1/43.**G.**
Don. 16/3—6/4/46.**G.**
Don. 13/4—6/5/49.**G.**
Don. 21/7—15/8/52.**G.**
Don. 3/4—18/5/57.**G.**
Don. 25/8/61. *Not Repaired.*

BOILERS:
1629 *(exJ4 745).*
7949 *(ex1069)* 30/3/35.
8450 *(ex3219)* 2/1/43.
8549 *(exC12 7356)* 6/5/49.
21918 *(new)* 15/8/52.

21846 *(ex68984)* 18/5/57.

SHEDS:
Ardsley.
Hornsey 28/9/52.
King's Cross 9/7/61.

RENUMBERED:
8931 20/1/46.
68931 6/5/49.

CONDEMNED: 25/8/61.
Cut up at Doncaster.

3233

Doncaster 1585.

To Traffic 8/3/24.

REPAIRS:
Don. 23/6—13/9/27.**G.**
Don. 8/3—5/4/30.**G.**
Don. 24/12/32—14/1/33.**G.**
Don. 13—20/2/37.**G.**
Don. 17/8—14/9/40.**G.**
Don. 4—24/12/43.**G.**
Don. 1—29/12/45.**G.**
Don. 11/4—14/5/48.**G.**
Don. 28/8—28/9/51.**G.**
Don. 3—27/8/54.**G.**
Don. 18/3—17/4/58.**G.**
Don. 12/12/61. *Not Repaired.*

BOILERS:
6956 *(exJ4 373).*
8673 *(new)* 14/1/33.
9252 *(ex8975)* 14/5/48.
21842 *(reno from 8554)* 28/9/51.
21802 *(ex68939)* 27/8/54.
21914 *(ex68964)* 17/4/58.

SHEDS:
Bradford.
Low Moor 12/1/58.
Copley Hill 20/8/61.

RENUMBERED:
8932 20/1/46.
68932 14/5/48.

CONDEMNED: 12/12/61.
Cut up at Doncaster.

3234

Doncaster 1588.

To Traffic 15/3/24.

REPAIRS:
Don. 26/5—30/7/27.**G.**
Don. 4—25/7/31.**G.**

Don. 12/5—2/6/34.**G.**
Don. 23/10—6/11/37.**G.**
Don. 9/11—7/12/40.**G.**
Don. 30/10—20/11/43.**G.**
Don. 12/8—7/10/47.**G.**
Don. 5—22/4/49.**C/L.**
Don. 5/6—6/7/51.**G.**
Don. 9/8—2/9/54.**G.**
Don. 9/11—5/12/57.**G.**
Don. 12/12/61. *Not Repaired.*

BOILERS:
6991 *(exE1 887).*
8483 *(exJ55 3689)* 2/6/34.
8552 *(ex8902)* 7/10/47.
21827 *(reno from 10517)* 6/7/51.
21829 *(ex68975)* 2/9/54.
21896 *(ex68916)* 5/12/57.

SHEDS:
Bradford.
Low Moor 12/1/58.
Wakefield 1/5/60.

RENUMBERED:
8933 20/1/46.
68933 22/4/49.

CONDEMNED: 12/12/61.
Cut up at Doncaster.

3235

Doncaster 1590.

To Traffic 29/3/24.

REPAIRS:
Don. 1—4/10/24.**L.**
After collision.
Don. 26/3—17/5/27.**G.**
Don. 16/8—20/9/30.**G.**
Don. 16—30/3/35.**G.**
Don. 11/3—1/4/39.**G.**
Don. 15/8—5/9/42.**G.**
Don. 27/10—24/11/45.**G.**
Don. 31/8—7/9/46.**L.**
Don. 12/10—19/11/48.**G.**
Don. 20/11—14/12/51.**G.**
Don. 9—17/2/54.**N/C.**
Don. 12—20/4/54.**N/C.**
Don. 19/1—18/2/55.**G.**
Don. 26/4—30/5/58.**G.**
Don. 8—19/7/63.**C/L.**

BOILERS:
6961 *(exE1 758).*
8511 *(exC12 4549)* 30/3/35.
8170 *(exC12 4019)* 5/9/42.
9824 *(new)* 19/11/48.
21848 *(reno fm. 8687)* 14/12/51.
21870 *(ex68970)* 18/2/55.
21943 *(exC12 67391)* 30/5/58.

SHEDS:
Ardsley.
Bradford ?/?/?.
Doncaster 13/2/31.
Ardsley 4/3/31.
Copley Hill 30/5/32.
Ardsley 19/9/32.
Hatfield 4/5/39.
Ardsley 13/10/39.
Bradford 5/3/44.
Low Moor 12/1/58.
Darlington 2/3/58.
Ardsley 2/8/59.

RENUMBERED:
8934 27/1/46.
68934 19/11/48.

CONDEMNED: 23/9/63.
Into Dar. for cut up 10/63 .

3236

Doncaster 1591.

To Traffic 26/4/24.

REPAIRS:
Don. 30/11/28—18/1/29.**G.**
Don. 20/12/30—24/1/31.**G.**
Don. 12/8—9/9/33.**G.**
Don. 13—27/7/35.**G.**
Don. 17—24/7/37.**G.**
Don. 16/9—14/10/39.**G.**
Don. 11/10—8/11/41.**G.**
Don. 26/2—18/3/44.**G.**
Don. 23/2—16/3/46.**G.**
Don. 27/10—5/12/47.**G.**
Don. 30/3—27/4/51.**G.**
Don. 5—28/5/52.**C/L.**
Don. 4/1—3/2/54.**C/H.**
Don. 25/7—19/8/55.**G.**
Don. 2—30/4/59.**G.**
Don. 28—31/1/63.**C/L.**

BOILERS:
7077 *(exE1 992).*
8672 *(new)* 27/7/35.
8304 *(ex3169)* 8/11/41.
21912 *(new)* 27/4/51.
21916 *(exC12 67383)* 19/8/55.
21963 *(ex 68987)* 30/4/59.

SHEDS:
Ardsley.
Gorton 7/11/25.
Immingham 18/1/29.
Annesley 13/10/46.
Colwick 22/1/50.
Ardsley 28/9/52.

RENUMBERED:
8935 27/1/46.
68935 27/4/51.

All seven were quickly fitted with the shunter's riding step and handrail across the base of the bunker as was the custom on the Scottish Area shunting engines.

Ex works 15th December 1928, No.1074 had been fitted with a Dederich speed indicator so that this engine could be tried on hump shunting at Whitemoor. The trials only lasted until 15th February 1929 as a more powerful locomotive was found to be needed and the speed indicator passed to T1 class No.1358.

(above) From 12th December 1929 to 24th December 1932, No.1068 was fitted with Neckar water softening apparatus.

(left) From a Light repair at Stratford No.8950 was ex works 24th June 1946 fitted with a 'Jay-Gee' smoke eliminator. This provided extra air draught when the firehole door was open, but it was taken off when this locomotive went to Doncaster for repair on 11th February 1949. Stratford, 24th June 1946.

3236 cont./
CONDEMNED: 23/9/63.
Into Dar. for cut up 10/63 .

_____

3237

Doncaster 1593.

To Traffic 26/4/24.

REPAIRS:
Don. 15/3—24/4/26.**H.**
Don. 20/12/26—5/3/27.**G.**
Don. 13/12/30—3/1/31.**G.**
Don. 1—15/4/33.**G.**
Don. 7—21/3/36.**G.**
Don. 24/3—11/4/36.**L.**
Don. 31/12/38—14/1/39.**G.**
Don. 11—25/1/41.**G.**
Don. 22/5—26/6/43.**G.**
Don. 13/10—10/11/45.**G.**
Don. 20/5—16/6/48.**G.**
Don. 23/5—18/6/52.**G.**
Don. 26/2—29/3/56.**G.**
Don. 26/4/61. *Not Repaired.*

BOILERS:
 7081 *(exD4 1318).*
 7815 *(exC12 4541)* 15/4/33.
 9506 *(new)* 10/11/45.
 21871 *(reno from 8767)* 18/6/52.
 21839 *(ex68930)* 29/3/56.

SHEDS:
Ardsley.
Sheffield 6/11/25.
Bradford 8/3/26.
Ardsley 2/2/31.
Stratford 14/2/31.
Immingham 9/4/34.
Frodingham 28/7/46.
Doncaster 28/9/46.
Hornsey 28/9/52.

RENUMBERED:
 8936 16/6/46.
 68936 16/6/48.

CONDEMNED: 26/4/61.
Cut up at Doncaster.

_____

3238

Doncaster 1596.

To Traffic 31/5/24.

REPAIRS:
Don. 20/6—15/9/27.**G.**
Don. 16/8—6/9/30.**G.**
Don. 23/9—14/10/33.**G.**
Don. 13—27/2/37.**G.**
Don. 8—22/6/40.**G.**

Don. 5/6—17/7/43.**G.**
Don. 9/2—9/3/46.**G.**
Don. 13/9—15/10/48.**G.**
Don. 5—6/10/60.**N/C.**
Don. 20/8—21/9/51.**G.**
Don. 6—31/8/54.**G.**
Don. 27/11—24/12/58.**G.**

BOILERS:
 7037 *(exE1 882).*
 8689 *(new)* 27/2/37.
 8486 *(ex3215)* 17/7/43.
 21841 *(reno from 8265)* 21/9/51.
 21805 *(ex68893)* 31/8/54.
 21901 *(ex68926)* 24/12/58.

SHEDS:
Ardsley.
St Margarets 7/10/25.
Ardsley 19/3/26.
Copley Hill 30/1/28.
Ardsley 15/9/57.
Mirfield 11/3/62.
Ardsley 29/4/62.

RENUMBERED:
 8937 2/6/46.
 68937 15/10/48.

CONDEMNED: 23/9/63.
Into Dar. for cut up 11/63 .

_____

3239

Doncaster 1597.

To Traffic 31/5/24.

REPAIRS:
Don. 18/8—29/10/27.**G.**
Don. 7—28/2/31.**G.**
Don. 16—30/3/35.**G.**
Don. 11/3—1/4/39.**G.**
Don. 1—15/3/41.**G.**
Don. 18/3—8/4/44.**G.**
Don. 18/5—1/6/46.**L.**
Don. 25/11/46—1/1/47.**G.**
Don. 23/10—13/11/47.**L.**
Don. 16/2—5/3/48.**L.**
Don. 22/7—26/8/49.**G.**
Don. 1/9—3/10/52.**G.**
Don. 4/4—5/5/56.**G.**
Don. 2/10/59. *Not Repaired.*

BOILERS:
 1628 *(ex ?).*
 8557 *(exC12 4541)* 30/3/35.
 8556 *(ex3175)* 15/3/41.
 8673 *(ex8932)* 26/8/49.
 21919 *(new)* 3/10/52

SHEDS:
Ardsley.
Neville Hill 8/10/25.

Ardsley 8/3/26.
Hatfield 27/4/39.
Ardsley 14/10/39.

RENUMBERED:
 8938 1/6/46.
 E8938 5/3/48.
 68938 26/8/49.

CONDEMNED: 5/10/59.
Cut up at Doncaster.

_____

3240

Doncaster 1599.

To Traffic 28/6/24.

REPAIRS:
Don. 20/5—16/7/27.**G.**
Don. 4—25/4/31.**G.**
Don. 12/5—2/6/34.**G.**
Don. 8/5—5/6/37.**G.**
Don. 28/6—26/7/41.**G.**
Don. 1—29/4/44.**G.**
Don. 16/2—21/3/47.**G.**
Don. 28/8—27/9/50.**G.**
Don. 1—24/2/54.**G.**
Don. 2—9/2/57.**C/L.**
Don. 14/12/57—16/1/58.**G.**

BOILERS:
 1610 *(exJ7 374).*
 8449 *(ex J55 3783)* 2/6/34.
 8513 *(ex3168)* 29/4/44.
 21802 *(reno fm. 10576)* 27/9/50.
 21888 *(ex68966)* 24/2/54.
 21915 *(ex68918)* 16/1/58.

SHEDS:
Ardsley.
Immingham 22/9/25.
Ardsley 29/3/26.
Copley Hill 16/11/34.
Ardsley 24/11/38.
Wakefield 22/2/59.

RENUMBERED:
 8939 16/6/46.
 68939 27/9/50.

CONDEMNED: 29/10/62.
Into Don. for cut up 19/12/62.

_____

583

Doncaster 1637.

To Traffic 18/3/26.

REPAIRS:
Don. 12/11—21/12/27.**L.**
Don. 8/11—14/12/29.**G.**

Don. 27/2—15/5/33.**G.**
Don. 30/12/36—20/1/37.**G.**
Don. 5/10—9/11/40.**G.**
Don. 23/10—13/11/43.**G.**
Don. 24/2—24/3/45.**G.**
Don. 15/2—19/3/48.**G.**
Don. 21/1—13/2/52.**G.**
Don. 14/2—10/3/55.**G.**
Don. 15—21/3/56.**G.**
Don. 3/9/58. *Not Repaired.*

BOILERS:
 7923 *(new).*
 8485 *(exC12 4546)* 20/1/37.
 9310 *(new)* 24/3/45.
 9821 *(new)* 19/3/48.
 21854 *(reno from 9507)* 13/2/52.
 21864 *(ex68905)* 10/3/55.

SHEDS:
Bradford.
Low Moor 12/1/58.

RENUMBERED:
 8940 21/7/46.
 68940 19/3/48.

CONDEMNED: 15/9/58.
Cut up at Doncaster.

_____

586

Doncaster 1638.

To Traffic 30/3/26.

REPAIRS:
Don. 20/5—27/6/30.**G.**
Don. 24/4—11/5/35.**G.**
Don. 6/5—3/6/39.**G.**
Don. 21/11—5/12/42.**G.**
Don. 19/1—9/2/46.**G.**
Don. 9/2—3/3/49.**G.**
Don. 28/8—29/9/52.**G.**
Don. 7/11—8/12/56.**G.**
Don. 13/12/61. *Not Repaired.*

BOILERS:
 7924 *(new).*
 8678 *(new)* 11/5/35.
 7815 *(ex8972)* 3/3/49.
 21880 *(reno from 9505)* 29/9/52.
 21856 *(ex68948)* 8/12/56.

SHEDS:
Bradford.
Ardsley 11/12/30.
Bradford 26/3/41.
Ardsley 19/4/53.
Darlington 18/5/58.
West Hartlepool 25/5/58.
Selby 14/6/59.
Ardsley 13/9/59.

586 cont./
RENUMBERED:
 8941 17/3/46.
 68941 3/3/49.

CONDEMNED: 13/12/61.
Cut up at Doncaster.

_____

588

Doncaster 1639.

To Traffic 7/4/26.

REPAIRS:
Don. 8/11—20/12/29.**G.**
Don. 5/10—25/11/32.**G.**
Don. 21/3—18/4/36.**G.**
Don. 6—27/1/40.**G.**
Don. 25/7—8/8/42.**G.**
Don. 29/12/45—26/1/46.**G.**
Don. 23/3—19/4/47.**L.**
Don. 2/3—24/3/49.**G.**
Don. 8—9/2/51.**N/C.**
Don. 10/11—3/12/52.**G.**
Don. 10/8—14/9/55.**G.**
Don. 19/9/58. *Not Repaired.*

BOILERS:
 7925 *(new).*
 8687 *(new)* 18/4/36.
 10516 *(new)* 24/3/49.
 21885 *(reno fm. 10518)* 3/12/52.
 21912 *(ex68935)* 14/9/55.

SHEDS:
Bradford.
Low Moor 12/1/58.
Middlesbrough 4/5/58.
Thornaby 1/6/58.

RENUMBERED:
 8942 17/3/46.
 68942 24/3/49.

CONDEMNED: 19/9/58.
Cut up at Doncaster.

_____

The original January 1914 design proved short of coal capacity and so the first ten built - those which became Part 1 - had a cage added above the bunker coal rails soon after construction.

During May and June 1945 the ten Part 1, Nos.3157 to 3164, 3166 and 3167, were renumbered 3180 to 3189 so that Class O6 LMS type 2-8-0s being built at Doncaster could take numbers 3157 to 3167. Woodford, 20th July 1946.

Beyond the addition of the cage, the Part 1 engines had no subsequent bunker alterations and the original four open coal rails were never fitted with plating. Colwick shed, 19th July 1958.

589

Doncaster 1640.

To Traffic 7/4/26.

REPAIRS:
Don. 8/1—26/2/30.**G.**
Don. 1/12/32—1/2/33.**G.**
Don. 23/5—19/6/36.**G.**
Don. 27/7—17/8/40.**G.**
Don. 10/4—15/5/43.**G.**
Don. 28/9—19/10/46.**G.**
Don. 7/8—16/9/49.**G.**
Don. 28/2—29/3/53.**G.**
Don. 5—25/7/55.**C/H.**
Don. 2/4—7/5/58.**G.**
Don. 29/10/60. Not Repaired.

BOILERS:
 7927 (new).
 8763 (new) 19/6/36.
 8766 (ex C12 7393) 16/9/49.
21890 (reno fm. 10516) 29/3/53.
21802 (ex68932) 7/5/58.

SHEDS:
Bradford.
Low Moor 12/1/58.

RENUMBERED:
 8943 21/7/46.
68943 16/9/49.

CONDEMNED: 20/2/61.
Cut up at Doncaster.

_____

591

Doncaster 1641.

To Traffic 16/4/26.

REPAIRS:
Don. 5/5—9/7/30.**G.**
Don. 25/8—5/10/33.**G.**
Don. 6—23/8/37.**G.**
Don. 8/2—1/3/41.**G.**
Don. 15/5—12/6/43.**G.**
Don. 17—24/7/43.**L.**
Don. 10—17/6/44.**G.**
Don. 12/11—11/12/47.**G.**
Don. 11/6—12/7/51.**G.**
Don. 15/9—13/10/54.**G.**
Don. 12/2—13/3/58.**G.**
Don. 18/9—10/10/59.**C/H.**
Don. 17/9/60. Not Repaired.

BOILERS:
 7926 (new).
 7929 (ex594) 23/8/37.
 8768 (ex8912) 11/12/47.
21828 (reno from 9104) 12/7/51.
21842 (ex68932) 13/10/54.

21897 (ex68951) 13/3/58.

SHEDS:
Bradford.
Ardsley 30/1/36.
Bradford 16/5/38.
Doncaster 28/5/50.
Bradford 9/7/50.
Low Moor 12/1/58.

RENUMBERED:
 8944 31/3/46.
68944 12/7/51.

CONDEMNED: 17/9/60.
Cut up at Doncaster.

_____

593

Doncaster 1642.

To Traffic 24/4/26.

REPAIRS:
Don. 13/1—1/3/30.**G.**
Don. 10/6—21/8/33.**G.**
Don. 8/12/36—6/1/37.**G.**
Don. 21/9—19/10/40.**G.**
Don. 4—18/3/44.**G.**
Don. 23/9—7/10/44.**G.**
Don. 13/6—20/7/48.**G.**
Don. 8—26/8/49.**C/L.**
Don. 10/8—4/9/51.**G.**
Don. 13/12/55—13/1/56.**G.**
Don. 21/4/61. Not Repaired.

BOILERS:
 7928 (new).
 7925 (ex588) 6/1/37.
 9309 (new) 18/3/44.
21840 (reno from 8768) 4/9/51.

SHEDS:
Copley Hill.
Doncaster 10/4/49.
Hornsey 28/9/52.

RENUMBERED:
 8945 31/3/46.
68945 17/7/48.

CONDEMNED: 21/4/61.
Cut up at Doncaster.

_____

594

Doncaster 1643.

To Traffic 30/4/26.

REPAIRS:
Don. 15/5—20/6/30.**G.**
Don. 30/10—13/12/33.**G.**

Don. 13/1—3/2/37.**G.**
Don. 9/11—7/12/40.**G.**
Don. 27/5—10/6/44.**G.**
Don. 2/5—2/6/48.**G.**
Don. 21/2—17/3/54.**G.**
Don. 15/8—26/9/58.**G.**
Don. 21/2/61. Not Repaired.

BOILERS:
 7929 (new).
 7927 (ex589) 3/2/37.
 8312 (ex8898) 2/6/48.
21946 (reno from 9108) 17/3/54.
21848 (ex68896) 26/9/58.

SHEDS:
Copley Hill.
Doncaster 10/4/49.
Mexborough 18/12/49.
Immingham 21/6/53.
Hornsey 3/4/55.

RENUMBERED:
 8946 31/3/46.
68946 2/6/48.

CONDEMNED: 23/2/61.
Cut up at Doncaster.

_____

596

Doncaster 1644.

To Traffic 1/5/26.

REPAIRS:
Don. 29/8—27/9/29.**G.**
Don. 14/11/32—21/1/33.**G.**
Don. 11/2—9/3/35.**G.**
Don. 6/5—3/6/39.**G.**
Don. 16—30/1/43.**G.**
Don. 27/10—17/11/45.**G.**
Don. 6/3—1/4/49.**G.**
Don. 29/1—4/2/52.**N/C.**
Don. 23/9—17/10/52.**G.**
Don. 6/5—8/6/57.**G.**
Don. 24/11/60. Not Repaired.

BOILERS:
 7932 (new).
 7388 (ex1079) 9/3/35.
 8266 (ex2790) 3/6/39.
 9306 (new) 30/1/43.
10518 (new) 1/4/49.
21882 (reno fm. 8302) 17/10/52.
21940 (ex68915) 8/6/57.

SHED:
Ardsley.

RENUMBERED:
 8947 28/4/46.
68947 1/4/49.

CONDEMNED: 20/2/61.
Cut up at Doncaster.

_____

601

Doncaster 1645.

To Traffic 27/5/26.

REPAIRS:
Don. 22/8—21/9/29.**G.**
Don. 1/11—16/12/32.**G.**
Don. 18/7—15/8/35.**G.**
Don. 4/11—2/12/39.**G.**
Don. 24/10—7/11/42.**G.**
Don. 28/4—19/5/45.**G.**
Don. 22/3—27/4/48.**G.**
Don. 27/1—22/2/52.**G.**
Don. 16/10—17/11/56.**G.**
Don. 15/11/61. Not Repaired.

BOILERS:
 7930 (new).
 8068 (ex C12 4514) 15/8/35.
 9304 (ex606) 19/5/45.
21856 (reno from 9644) 22/2/52.
21917 (ex68979) 17/11/56.

SHEDS:
Ardsley.
Woodford Halse 17/2/33.
Ardsley 26/2/35.
Darlington 18/5/58.
Middlesbrough 25/5/58.
Thornaby 1/6/58.
Selby 7/12/58.
Copley Hill 13/9/59.
Low Moor 27/9/59.

RENUMBERED:
 8948 28/4/46.
68948 24/4/48.

CONDEMNED: 15/11/61.
Cut up at Doncaster.

_____

603

Doncaster 1646.

To Traffic 11/6/26.

REPAIRS:
Don. 28/10—4/12/29.**G.**
Don. 14/8—2/10/33.**G.**
Don. 24/2—1/4/37.**G.**
Don. 7/9—5/10/40.**G.**
Don. 28/8—11/9/43.**G.**
Don. 2/12/46—4/1/47.**G.**
Don. 17/7—22/8/50.**G.**
Str. 23/8—2/10/54.**G.**
Don. 14/4/59. Not Repaired.

The next twenty, built as J51, were fitted with a longer bunker, but were only then provided with three coal rails. These were still open until after at least sixteen of the thirty had been rebuilt to Class J50. Copley Hill.

Beginning in 1931, all the seventy-eight Part 2 and Part 3 engines had steel plating put inside the rails to help stop spillage of the smaller coal which was then having to be used. Ardsley, 27th June 1937.

The first ten engines built with 4ft 5in. boilers, Nos.221 to 230 (which were the last built by the GNR) also had three rails of rectangular section. They had plating added from 1931.

On the first ten built by the LNER, Nos.3231 to 3240, there were also three open coal rails but the section was half-round instead of rectangular and the thirty-eight standard engines built 1926 to 1930 also had half round section.

(above) When building was begun again in 1938, coal rails were absent, the bunker being built up and incorporating a hopper shaped top. Two steps were fitted on each side and there was a short hand grip by the top of the cab opening, as had been fitted on all the earlier engines. Stratford, 13th October 1949.

From 1959 some, but not all of the fourteen engines with hopper bunker had handrails added to each side and across the back on the hopper portion.

The height of the tanks did not permit handrails along the side of the boiler but a short horizontal grip was fitted on each side of the smokebox.

This hand grip assumed a variety of positions. Towards the end of the LNER some had it placed diagonally and the illustration at the bottom of page 165 shows one almost vertical. Stratford.

(below) Many did manage to keep the hand grip in its original position through to their withdrawal in the 1960's. Although retaining the horizontal grip, No.68917 latterly had it placed much higher than on the others (see also page 166, top).

Through to the 1930 built engines, the redundant pairs of lamp irons to suit GNR lamp codes were still fitted when engines were new, but during the 1930's the useless irons were taken off the English shedded engines. Annesley shed.

603 cont./
BOILERS:
7931 *(new)*.
7943 *(ex1037)* 1/4/37.
8447 *(ex3211)* 11/9/43.
8315 *(ex8964)* 22/8/50.
21906 *(ex68899)* 2/10/54.

SHEDS:
Ardsley.
Neasden 27/5/51.
Hornsey 27/1/52.

RENUMBERED:
8949 16/6/46.
68949 22/8/50.

CONDEMNED: 14/4/59.
Cut up at Doncaster.

609

Doncaster 1647.

To Traffic 5/8/26.

REPAIRS:
Don. 28/10—2/12/29.**G**.
Don. 15/2—6/5/32.**G**.
Don. 12/6—28/7/34.**G**.
Don. 2/5—17/6/37.**G**.
Don. 3/2—2/3/40.**G**.
Don. 27/3—17/4/43.**G**.
Don. 22/9—6/10/45.**G**.
Str. 7—24/6/46.**L**.
Jay-Gee smoke eliminator fitted.
Don. 11—25/2/49.**G**.
*Jay-Gee smoke eliminator
removed.*
Don. 30/11/49—20/1/50.**C/H**.
Str. 2—3/5/51.**N/C**.
Don. 2/12/51—1/1/52.**G**.
Str. 15/12/54—15/1/55.**G**.
Don. 18/6—26/7/58.**G**.
Don. 23/9/61. *Not Repaired*.

BOILERS:
7933 *(new)* .
9307 *(new)* 17/4/43.
9109 *(ex8988)* 25/2/49.
9644 *(ex8966)* 20/1/50.
21850 *(reno from 9309)* 1/1/52.
21965 *(reno from 9249)* 15/1/55.
21902 *(exC12 67380)* 26/7/58.

SHEDS:
Ardsley.
Doncaster 31/3/27.
Ardsley 6/5/27.
Immingham 7/12/29.
Doncaster 17/6/37.

Stratford 16/3/46.
*On loan to Cricklewood (LMR)
four w/e 12/6/48, returned to
Stratford four w/e 7/8/48.*
Immingham 29/1/56.
Colwick 8/7/56.
Hornsey 14/2/60.
King's Cross 9/7/61.

RENUMBERED:
8950 13/4/46.
68950 25/2/49.

CONDEMNED: 23/9/61.
Cut up at Doncaster.

610

Doncaster 1648.

To Traffic 5/8/26.

REPAIRS:
Don. 9/2—30/3/29.**G**.
Don. 10/6—2/9/32.**G**.
Don. 4—27/6/36.**G**.
Don. 1—15/6/40.**G**.
Don. 10—24/7/43.**G**.
Don. 12—26/10/46.**G**.
Don. 22/11—23/12/49.**G**.
Don. 10—19/7/51.**C/L**.
Don. 13/7—10/8/53.**G**.
Don. 1—7/2/57.**N/C**.
Don. 14/11—14/12/57.**G**.
Don. 12—30/6/59.**N/C**.
Don. 30/6/61. *Not Repaired*.

BOILERS:
7935 *(new)*.
8764 *(new)* 27/6/36.
8515 *(exC12 4544)* 26/10/46.
8763 *(ex8943)* 23/12/49.
21897 *(reno from 9110)* 10/8/53.
21905 *(ex68890)* 14/12/57.

SHEDS:
Ardsley.
Keadby 16/8/28.
Ardsley 30/3/29.
Copley Hill 15/5/30.
Ardsley 2/7/30.
Copley Hill 14/7/30.
Ardsley 21/9/30.
Copley Hill 13/6/33.
Ardsley 31/8/33.
Darlington 18/5/58.
West Hartlepool 8/6/58.
Ardsley 11/6/61.

RENUMBERED:
8951 28/4/46.

68951 23/12/49.

CONDEMNED: 3/7/61.
Cut up at Doncaster.

616

Doncaster 1649.

To Traffic 24/7/26.

REPAIRS:
Cow. 26/10—?/11/32.**G**.
Cow. ?/?—3/4/35.**H**.
Cow. 8—22/8/36.**H**.
Cow. ?/?—19/8/39.**G**.
Cow. 14/3—11/4/42.**G**.
Cow. ?/?—25/11/44.**H**.
Cow. 27/5—20/6/47.**G**.
Cow. 20/12/49—12/1/50.**G**.
Cow. 27/1—14/2/53.**G**.
Inv. 20—24/4/54.**C/L**.
Cow. 22/11—4/12/54.**C/L**.
Cow. 21/9—29/11/55.**H/I**.

BOILERS:
7934 *(new)*.
7948 *(ex1069)* 11/4/42.
7944 *(ex8956)* 20/6/47.
21983 *(ex68958)* 14/2/53.

SHEDS:
Eastfield.
St Margarets 6/4/46.
Eastfield 13/1/52.

RENUMBERED:
8952 12/4/46.
68952 12/1/50.

CONDEMNED: 17/8/60.
Cut up at Cowlairs 3/9/60.

617

Doncaster 1650.

To Traffic 6/8/26.

REPAIRS:
Cow. ?/12/32—9/1/33.**G**.
Cow. ?/?—3/10/35.**H**.
Cow. 20/2—28/4/37.**H**.
Drop grate fitted.
Cow. 25/4—9/5/42.**G**.
Cow. ?/?—15/4/44.**H**.
Cow. 18/8—1/9/45.**L**.
Cow. ?/?—3/4/46.**H**.
Cow. 24/2—10/5/47.**G**.
Cow. 24/10—2/12/50.**G**.

Cow. 3—25/6/53.**L/I**.
Cow. 2/8/55.**N/C**.
Cow. 23/11—17/12/55.**G**.
Cow. 13/6—3/8/57.**L/I**.

BOILERS:
7936 *(new)*.
7934 *(ex616)* 9/5/42.
7936 *(ex8954)* 2/12/50.
7936 reno.21981 25/6/53.
21984 *(ex68954)* 17/12/55.

SHEDS:
Eastfield.
Polmadie 8/5/57.

RENUMBERED:
8953 13/4/46.
68953 21/8/48.

CONDEMNED: 24/7/59.
Cut up at Cowlairs 9/1/60.

618

Doncaster 1651.

To Traffic 13/8/26.

REPAIRS:
Cow. ?/?—30/9/33.**G**.
Cow. ?/?—2/11/35.**G**.
Cow. ?/?—14/5/38.**G**.
Cow. ?/?—18/8/39.**H**.
Cow. ?/?—4/9/40.**H**.
Cow. ?/?—12/5/42.**L**.
Cow. 21/11—5/12/42.**G**.
Cow. ?/?—8/9/44.**L**.
Cow. 11/7—1/8/46.**L**.
Cow. 24/9—16/10/48.**G**.
Cow. 9/1—8/2/51.**L/I**.
Cow. 4/2—13/3/54.**G**.
Cow. 29—31/3/54.**N/C**.

BOILERS:
7937 *(new)*.
7944 *(ex Don. 1041)* 14/5/38.
7936 *(ex678)* 5/12/42.
7940 *(ex8957)* 16/10/48.
7940 reno.21984 8/2/51.
21987 *(ex68957)* 13/3/54.

SHED:
Eastfield.

RENUMBERED:
8954 12/4/46.
68954 16/10/48.

CONDEMNED: 18/8/60.
Cut up at Cowlairs 3/9/60.

WORKS CODES:- Cow - Cowlairs. Dar - Darlington. Don - Doncaster. Ghd - Gateshead. Gor - Gorton. Inv - Inverurie. Kit - Kittybrewster. RSH - Robert, Stephenson & Hawthorn. Str - Stratford. Yk - York.
REPAIR CODES:- **C/H** - Casual Heavy. **C/L** - Casual Light. **G** - General. **H** - Heavy. **H/I** - Heavy Intermediate. **L** - Light. **L/I** - Light Intermediate. **N/C** - Non-Classified.

The seven engines shedded in Scotland, and maintained by Cowlairs, all kept the double lamp irons at the front and rear through to withdrawals in July/August 1960. Eastfield, 21st July 1960.

From the introduction of the LNER design in April 1926 Ross 'pop' safety valves were standardised, and no base cover was provided. Eastfield.

621

Doncaster 1652.

To Traffic 28/8/26.

REPAIRS:
Cow. ?/11—14/12/33.**G.**
Cow. 6/6—16/7/36.**H.**
Cow. ?/?—21/4/39.**G.**
Cow. 16/8—20/9/41.**H.**
Cow. ?/?—29/1/44.**H.**
Cow. 14/2—13/3/47.**G.**
Cow. 17—26/6/48.**L/I.**
Cow. 8/8—16/9/49.**L/I.**
Cow. 16/11—8/12/51.**G.**
Cow. 31/3—8/5/54.**L/I.**

BOILERS:
7938 *(new).*
7941 *(ex8958)* 13/3/47.
21980 *(ex68953)* 8/12/51.

SHED:
Eastfield.

RENUMBERED:
8955 4/5/46.
68955 26/6/48.

CONDEMNED: 8/12/59.
Cut up at Cowlairs 30/1/60.

_____

622

Doncaster 1653.

To Traffic 3/9/26.

REPAIRS:
Cow. 3—25/2/33.**G.**
Cow. 4/7—14/8/36.**H.**
Cow. 20/8—10/9/38.**H.**
Cow. ?/?—4/1/41.**G.**
Cow. ?/?—19/12/42.**G.**
Cow. 8—31/5/47.**G.**
Cow. 31/1—18/2/50.**L/I.**
Cow. 10—23/10/51.**H/I.**
Cow. 31/3—26/4/53.**G.**
Cow. 20/6—9/7/55.**L/I.**

BOILERS:
7939 *(new).*
7944 *(ex618)* 19/12/42.
7938 *(ex8955)* 31/5/47.
7938 reno.21982 23/10/51.
21986 *(ex68952)* 26/4/53.

SHED:
Eastfield.

RENUMBERED:
8956 28/4/46.
68956 18/2/50.

CONDEMNED: 17/8/60.
Cut up at Cowlairs 27/8/60.

_____

635

Doncaster 1654.

To Traffic 24/9/26.

REPAIRS:
Cow. ?/11/31—?/1/32.**G.**
Cow. ?/?—16/8/34.**?.**
Cow. 9/1—20/2/37.**H.**
Cow. 2/7—4/8/38.**H.**
Cow. ?/?—13/1/40.**H.**
Cow. 16/11/40—1/3/41.**H.**
Cow. ?/?—7/8/43.**H.**
Cow. 24/2—10/3/45.**H.**
Cow. ?/?—7/6/46.**L.**
Cow. 15/10—13/11/47.**G.**
Cow. 9—27/5/50.**G.**
Cow. 11/11—12/12/53.**G.**
Cow. 17—29/1/55.**C/L.**
Cow. 4/2—9/3/57.**H/I.**

BOILERS:
7940 *(new).*
7948 *(ex8952)* 13/11/47.
21982 *(ex68956)* 12/12/53.

SHED:
Eastfield.

RENUMBERED:
8957 28/4/46.
68957 27/5/50.

CONDEMNED: 23/8/60.
Cut up at Cowlairs 10/9/60.

_____

636

Doncaster 1655.

To Traffic 27/10/26.

REPAIRS:
Cow. ?/10—?/11/31.**G.**
Cow. ?/10—?/11/33.**G.**
Cow. 4—18/4/36.**H.**
Cow. ?/?—4/3/39.**H.**
Cow. 21/6—2/8/41.**H.**
Cow. ?/?—10/7/43.**H.**
Cow. 31/1—28/2/46.**G.**
Cow. 13/5—4/6/48.**G.**
Cow. 12—30/12/49.**H/I.**
Cow. 20/12/51—4/2/52.**G.**
Cow. 4/2—5/3/55.**H/I.**
Cow. 8—12/3/55.**N/C.**
Cow. 19/11—21/12/57.**G.**

BOILERS:
7941 *(new).*

7939 *(ex622)* 28/2/46.
21985 *(ex68955)* 4/2/52.
21981 *(ex68953)* 21/12/57.

SHEDS:
Eastfield.
Polmadie 8/5/57.

RENUMBERED:
8958 28/4/46.
68958 4/6/48.

CONDEMNED: 21/3/60.
Cut up at Cowlairs 14/5/60.

_____

1037

Doncaster 1656.

To Traffic 16/11/26.

REPAIRS:
Don. 14/7—5/9/30.**G.**
Don. 14/3—6/6/33.**G.**
Don. 23/2—20/3/37.**G.**
Don. 1—22/3/41.**G.**
Don. 13/11—11/12/43.**G.**
Don. 9/11—7/12/46.**G.**
Don. 14/3/47.**N/C.**
Don. 11/9—14/10/49.**G.**
Don. 16—17/1/51.**N/C.**
Don. 9/2—6/3/53.**G.**
Don. 31/1—23/2/57.**G.**
Don. 31/8/61. *Not Repaired.*

BOILERS:
7943 *(new).*
8301 *(exC12 4517)* 20/3/37.
9308 *(ex8982)* 14/10/49.
21923 *(new)* 6/3/53.
21936 *(new)* 23/2/57.

SHEDS:
Bradford.
Ardsley 6/10/57.
Darlington 18/5/58.
West Auckland 25/5/58.
Darlington 18/1/59.
Wakefield 19/7/59.
Low Moor 1/5/60.

RENUMBERED:
8959 27/1/46.
68959 14/10/49.

CONDEMNED: 31/8/61.
Cut up at Doncaster.

_____

1041

Doncaster 1657.

To Traffic 24/11/26.

REPAIRS:
Don. 8/1—15/2/30.**G.**
Don. 7/9—16/10/33.**G.**
Don. 17/11—4/12/37.**G.**
Don. 12/12/42—9/1/43.**G.**
Don. 29/9—20/10/45.**G.**
Don. 24/4—26/5/48.**G.**
Don. 13/7—8/8/52.**G.**
Don. 2—30/3/55.**G.**
Don. 15/1—6/2/58.**G.**
Don. 25/7/61. *Not Repaired.*

BOILERS:
7944 *(new).*
8270 *(ex2794)* 4/12/37.
8265 *(ex spare & 1079)* 9/1/43.
9505 *(new)* 20/10/45.
21877 *(reno from 9313)* 8/8/52.
21818 *(ex68906)* 30/3/55.
21948 *(ex68893)* 6/2/58.

SHEDS:
Bradford.
Ardsley 20/2/33.
Tuxford 3/3/38.
Ardsley 12/12/41.
Doncaster 28/11/49.
Mexborough 18/12/49.
Doncaster 15/10/50.
Frodingham 30/4/51.
Doncaster 15/6/58.
Hornsey 26/10/58.
King's Cross 9/7/61.

RENUMBERED:
8960 20/1/46.
68960 26/5/48.

CONDEMNED: 25/7/61.
Cut up at Doncaster.

_____

1045

Doncaster 1658.

To Traffic 29/11/26.

REPAIRS:
Don. 16/7—30/8/30.**G.**
Don. 26/6—29/8/33.**G.**
Don. 27/4—16/6/37.**G.**
Don. 1—15/3/41.**G.**
Don. 4—25/3/44.**G.**
Don. 30/3—13/4/45.**L.**
Don. 20—27/7/46.**L.**
Don. 20/11—12/12/47.**G.**
Don. 11/7—3/8/51.**G.**
Don. 26/3—1/5/56.**G.**
Don. 3/8—2/9/60.**G.**
To Service Stock 16/9/62.

BOILERS:
7946 *(new).*
8762 *(ex8915)* 12/12/47.

Cowlairs managed to find base covers for two of the engines it maintained, No.618 having a circular type in this August 1935 photograph (*see* also page 170, bottom and page 171, bottom). Cowlairs works.

From 12th August 1932 to 3rd December 1934 No.1079 had a boiler fitted with Ramsbottom safety valves and this was also used by No.596 from 9th March 1935 to 6th May 1939. The only other standard J50 not to have 'pops' was No.1058 from 10th February 1932 to 16th December 1935.

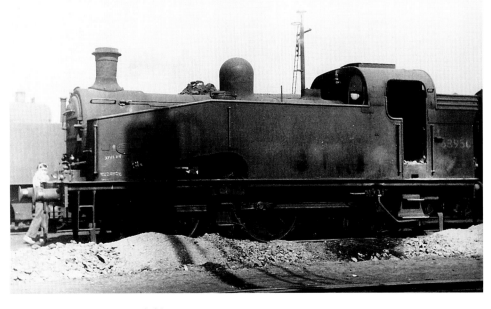

No.68950 in this 15th June 1958 photograph was an oddity because on a 1941 built boiler the 'pops' were almost completely hidden by a cut-down Ramsbottom cover. Note that the injector was still in its original position ahead of the cab footstep. Colwick, 15th June 1958.

The first fifty originally had faceplate injectors and when these were changed to under the footplate position they were usually fitted to the rear of the

At its last repair, ex works 16th January 1958, No.68939 got tanks with snaphead, instead of the customary countersunk rivets. Note that it had also been fitted with screw couplings. Wakefield, 8th July 1961.

(below) As built, and at the end of the LNER, all were 8ft 8in. wide across the footsteps.

Commencing with No.68965, ex Doncaster works 16th May 1952, the width across the footsteps was reduced to 8ft 6in. to make them more acceptable on London Transport widened lines workings. Seventy-two of the class were so altered including a number shedded only in the West Riding. Doncaster shed.

Withdrawals began on 15th September 1958 with No.68940 so that some never acquired the BR crest. Apart from those transferred to Departmental use, the last in traffic were ten to 23rd September 1963 - Nos.68892, 68904, 68908, 68922, 68934, 68935, 68937, 68965, 68977 and 68988. Two from Copley Hill, four from Wakefield and four from Ardsley, so that throughout from January 1914 to September 1963 they justified their name of the 'Ardsley tanks'. Doncaster works scrap yard, 16th August 1959.

1045 cont./
21833 *(reno from 8449)* 3/8/51.
21871 *(ex68936)* 1/5/56.
21893 *(ex68925)* 2/9/60.
21893 reno. S.B.4525 16/9/62.

SHEDS:
Bradford.
Doncaster 16/4/50.
Hornsey 28/9/52.
New England 9/7/61.
Doncaster 3/6/62.
Doncaster Works 16/9/62.

RENUMBERED:
 8961 20/1/46.
68961 3/8/51.
DEPT'L No.14 16/9/62.

WITHDRAWN: 16/9/62.
CONDEMNED: 19/9/65.
*Sold for scrap to T.W. Ward,
Beighton, 9/65.*

_____

1058

Doncaster 1659.

To Traffic 6/12/26.

REPAIRS:
Don. 13/7—3/8/29.**G.**
Don. 13/1—10/2/32.**G.**
Don. 9—23/7/34.**G.**
Don. 16—31/12/35.**G.**
Don. 8—22/10/38.**G.**
Don. 19/4—10/5/41.**G.**
Cow. 11/11—8/12/43.**H.**
Cow. 18/12/43—7/3/44.**L.**
*Sent to Stranraer engine shed for
return to LNER 29/5/45.*
Don. 18/5—22/6/46.**H.**
Don. 3—22/1/49.**G.**
Don. 30/10—22/11/51.**G.**
Don. 23/5—18/6/54.**G.**
Don. 1/9—5/10/57.**G.**
Don. 16/6/61. *Not Repaired.*

BOILERS:
 7945 *(new)*.
 7039 *(exC12 4549)* 10/2/32.
 7930 *(ex601)* 31/12/35.
 8670 *(exJ4 4112)* 22/1/49.
21846 *(reno fm. 9307)* 22/11/51.
21951 *(reno from 9306)* 18/6/54.
21961 *(ex68899)* 5/10/57.

SHEDS:
Ardsley.
March 23/4/28.
Immingham 3/8/29.
Keadby 2/12/29.
Frodingham 12/6/32.
King's Cross 28/8/39.

Hornsey 21/4/40.
Doncaster 27/5/40.
WD No.1 Military Port (Faslane)
17/2/42.
WD No.2 Military Port (Cairn-
ryan) 12/5/42.
Immingham 29/5/45.
Frodingham 22/12/46.
Doncaster 25/1/59.

RENUMBERED:
 8962 27/1/46.
68962 22/1/49.

CONDEMNED: 16/6/61.
Cut up at Doncaster.

_____

1063

Doncaster 1660.

To Traffic 10/12/26.

REPAIRS:
Don. 21/2—23/4/29.**G.**
Don. 13/6—26/7/30.**G.**
Don. 22/4—15/7/33.**G.**
Don. 3—31/12/35.**G.**
Don. 1—18/7/38.**G.**
Don. 12/4—3/5/41.**G.**
Don. 18/12/43—15/1/44.**G.**
Don. 25/5—22/6/46.**G.**
Don. 16/6—22/7/49.**G.**
Don. 20/2—14/3/52.**G.**
Str. 27/5—23/7/55.**G.**
Don. 23/11—6/12/56.**N/C.**
Don. 20/10—3/12/58.**G.**
Don. 13/2/62. *Not Repaired.*

BOILERS:
 7947 *(new)*.
 7952 *(ex1079)* 15/7/33.
 7967 *(ex1074)* 18/7/38.
 8266 *(ex8973)* 22/7/49.
21858 *(reno from 8674)* 14/3/52.
21966 *(reno from 8315)* 23/7/55.
21827 *(ex68892)* 3/12/58.

SHEDS:
Ardsley.
Keadby 10/2/28.
Langwith Junction 20/4/29.
Keadby 6/7/29.
Frodingham 12/6/32.
King's Cross 29/8/39.
Hornsey 21/4/40.
Sheffield 25/5/40.
Doncaster 14/5/42.
Stratford 14/7/46.
Immingham 29/1/56.
Doncaster 29/7/56.
Frodingham 13/1/57.
Doncaster 3/5/59.
Ardsley 30/7/61.

Low Moor 7/1/62.

RENUMBERED:
 8963 20/1/46.
68963 22/7/49.

CONDEMNED: 13/2/62.
Cut up at Doncaster.

_____

1068

Doncaster 1661.

To Traffic 14/12/26.

REPAIRS:
Don. 13/4—21/5/29.**G.**
Don. 9/9—12/12/29.**H.**
*Neckar water softening appara-
tus fitted.*
Don. 24/12/32—8/3/33.**G.**
Neckar apparatus removed.
Don. 15/8—19/9/35.**G.**
Don. 14—29/8/38.**G.**
Don. 5—26/4/41.**G.**
Don. 6—13/6/42.**L.**
Don. 29/1—19/2/44.**G.**
Don. 24/12/46—25/1/47.**G.**
Don. 15/12/49—20/1/50.**G.**
Don. 9/5—5/6/52.**G.**
Don. 29/12/54—21/1/55.**G.**
Don. 19/2—18/3/58.**G.**
Don. 1/10/62. *Not Repaired.*

BOILERS:
 7948 *(new)*.
 7965 *(ex1086)* 8/3/33.
 7952 *(ex1063)* 29/8/38.
 8315 *(ex8966)* 25/1/47.
 9305 *(ex8969)* 20/1/50.
21869 *(reno from 9103)* 5/6/52.
21914 *(ex68900)* 21/1/55.
21818 *(ex68960)* 18/3/58.

SHEDS:
Ardsley.
Immingham 7/10/27.
Lincoln 2/1/30.
Keadby 20/1/30.
Frodingham 12/6/32.
Doncaster 25/1/59.
Wakefield 23/7/61.
Ardsley 30/7/61.
Low Moor 7/1/62.

RENUMBERED:
 8964 27/1/46.
68964 20/1/50.

CONDEMNED: 1/10/62.
Cut up at Doncaster.

_____

1069

Doncaster 1662.

To Traffic 20/12/26.

REPAIRS:
Don. 22/7—31/8/29.**G.**
Don. 19/10—28/11/31.**G.**
Don. 22/1—17/3/34.**G.**
Don. 19/11—11/12/37.**G.**
Don. 28/12/37—8/1/38.**L.**
Don. 13/7—3/8/40.**G.**
Don. 3—24/4/43.**G.**
Don. 4/8—1/9/45.**G.**
Don. 1/7—25/8/49.**G.**
Don. 17/4—16/5/52.**G.**
Don. 1/2—3/3/56.**G.**
Don. 23/7—21/8/59.**G.**

BOILERS:
 7949 *(new)*.
 7948 *(ex1068)* 17/3/34.
 8150 *(ex1082)* 3/8/40.
 9313 *(new)* 1/9/45.
21866 *(reno from 9102)* 16/5/52.
21920 *(ex68919)* 3/3/56.
21916 *(ex68935)* 21/8/59.

SHEDS:
Ardsley.
Keadby 24/11/27.
Immingham 24/6/29.
Stratford 17/3/34.
Immingham 29/1/56.
Frodingham 25/11/56.
Doncaster 25/1/59.
Ardsley 30/7/61.
Mirfield 11/3/62.
Ardsley 29/4/62.

RENUMBERED:
 8965 20/1/46.
68965 25/8/49.

CONDEMNED: 23/9/63.
Cut up at Darlington 11/63.

_____

1070

Doncaster 1663.

To Traffic 20/12/26.

REPAIRS:
Don. 20/8—7/9/29.**G.**
Don. 13/12/32—2/3/33.**G.**
Don. 2—17/11/36.**G.**
Don. 28/9—26/10/40.**G.**
Don. 17—31/7/43.**G.**
Don. 21/9—5/10/46.**G.**
Don. 21/12/49—20/1/50.**G.**
Don. 5—14/1/53.**N/C.**
Don. 16/8—18/9/53.**G.**

164

On 22nd November 1960 No.68911 was withdrawn but instead of being scrapped it was transferred on 15th February 1961 to use in Doncaster locomotive works and renumbered No.10 Departmental Locomotive but it kept its No.68911 smokebox plate and also its 56C (Copley Hill) allocation plate. Eventually condemned on 30th May 1965, it was sold in July 1965 for cutting up by Thos.W.Ward at their Beighton yard. Note that for the sharp curves in the works it was fitted with GCR buffers having oval heads.

No.68914 was withdrawn on 12th November 1960 from Ardsley which had been its only shed since it was built in July 1919 as GNR No.215. On 15th February 1961 it became No.11 Departmental Locomotive keeping its 68914 smokebox plate but the shed allocation plate was taken off. A short handrail was fitted on the smokebox door *above* the number plate. It too got GCR type buffers and was also condemned 30th may 1965, being sold for scrap to the same yard as No.68911. Note it got small circular rear windows whereas No.68911 had kept large windows but had them partially plated. The smokebox hand grip was also set at an unusual angle. As a Doncaster works shunter it had acquired one of the special lamps used by repaired steam engines on main line trial trips. The plate read 'Return to Weigh House Plant Works Doncaster'.

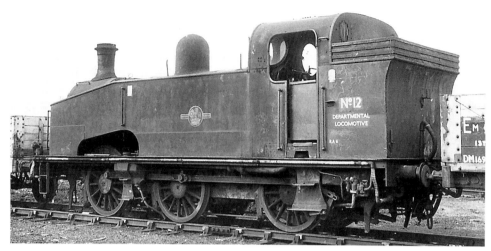

On 16th September 1962 five J50, Nos.68917, 68928, 68961, 68971 and 68976 were all withdrawn from traffic and transferred to Departmental Stock for use in Doncaster works. No.68917 became No.12 and kept its GNR buffers and smokebox number plate until condemned 30th May 1965. In July 1965 it was also sold for scrap to T.W.Ward at Beighton.

No.68928 became No.13 and kept GNR buffers also smokebox plate but its shed plate was taken off. It was condemned 30th May 1965 and sold to the Beighton yard. Note it has acquired (by chance) a Great Eastern white disc, probably left on one of that line's engines cut up by Doncaster works.

No.14 had been No.68961 and outlasted all the others as it was not condemned until 19th September 1965 thus bringing J50 class to its end.

In works use No.14 kept its 68961 smokebox number plate and its 34B plate although it had left Hornsey on 9th July 1961 for New England and then went to Doncaster shed on 3rd June 1962. It also retained the Group Standard buffers and drawhook fitted when new in November 1926.

Transferred from traffic to Departmental on 16th September 1962 and allocated No.15, the renumbering had still to be done when this 21st July 1963 photograph was taken. Although it had made the same shed transfers, on the same dates, as No.68961 it had been duly fitted with a 36A Doncaster shed plate. Doncaster works, 21st July 1963.

1070 cont./
*For Doncaster Works Centenary
Exhibition.*
Don. 21/5—20/6/58.**G.**
Str. 2—20/11/59.**N/C.**
Don. 1/8/61. *Not Repaired.*

BOILERS:
7950 *(new).*
8315 *(exC12 4513)* 17/11/36.
9644 *(new)* 5/10/46.
9643 *(ex8904)* 20/1/50.
9643 reno.21888 14/1/53.
21942 *(reno from 8678)* 18/9/53.
21945 *(exC12 67395)* 20/6/58.

SHEDS:
Ardsley.
Mexborough 16/12/27.
Ardsley 2/5/29.
Copley Hill 2/6/37.
Ardsley 27/9/37.
Hornsey 4/3/56.
King's Cross 9/7/61.

RENUMBERED:
8966 20/1/46.
68966 20/1/50.

CONDEMNED: 1/8/61.
Cut up at Doncaster.

_____

1074

Doncaster 1664.

To Traffic 20/1/27.

REPAIRS:
Don. 8/11—15/12/28.**G.**
Deuta speed indicator fitted.
Don. 26/11/30—14/2/31.**G.**
Don. 25/10—24/11/34.**G.**
Don. 27/2—31/3/38.**G.**
Don. 9/11—7/12/40.**G.**
Don. 22/5—12/6/43.**G.**
Str. 10—15/2/46.**L.**
Don. 29/10/46—16/1/47.**G.**
Don. 29/8—28/9/49.**G.**
Don. 31/8—9/10/52.**G.**
Str. 30/10—3/12/55.**G.**

BOILERS:
7951 *(new).*
8484 *(new)* 14/2/31.
7967 *(ex1082)* 24/11/34.
7945 *(ex1086)* 31/3/38.
8267 *(ex8976)* 28/9/49.
21881 *(reno from 8512)* 9/10/52.
21858 *(ex68963)* 3/12/55.

SHEDS:
Ardsley.
Gorton 18/2/27.

March 15/12/28.
Keadby 8/2/29.
Immingham 28/3/31.
Stratford 7/7/31.
Immingham 29/1/56.
Colwick 2/9/56.

RENUMBERED:
8967 20/1/46.
68967 28/9/49.

CONDEMNED: 16/6/59.
Into Don. for cut up 16/6/59.

_____

1079

Doncaster 1665.

To Traffic 29/1/27.

REPAIRS:
Don. 26/6—15/8/29.**G.**
Don. 7/5—12/8/32.**G.**
Don. 3/12/34—3/1/35.**G.**
Don. 21/8—4/9/37.**G.**
Don. 27/5—1/6/38.**L.**
Spark arrestor fitted.
Don. 28/10—18/11/39.**G.**
Don. 20/12/41—17/1/42.**G.**
Don. 19/2—11/3/44.**G.**
Don. 23/3—20/4/46.**G.**
Don. 31/1—25/2/49.**G.**
Don. 9/10—2/11/51.**G.**
Don. 1—25/5/55.**G.**
Don. 26/4/61. *Not Repaired.*

BOILERS:
7952 *(new).*
7388 *(exJ55 3153A)* 12/8/32.
7947 *(ex1063)* 3/1/35.
8265 *(ex2789)* 4/9/37
7965 *(ex1068)* 18/11/39.
8155 *(exC12 4523)* 20/4/46.
9311 *(ex8981)* 25/2/49.
21845 *(reno from 9251)* 2/11/51.
21804 *(ex68980)* 25/5/55.

SHEDS:
Ardsley.
Immingham 16/9/27.
Keadby ?/11/27.
Frodingham 12/6/32.
Immingham 17/9/32.
Woodford Halse 17/2/33.
Immingham 1/3/35.
Frodingham 22/12/46.
Hornsey 19/10/52.

RENUMBERED:
8968 27/1/46.
68968 25/2/49.

CONDEMNED: 26/4/61.
Cut up at Doncaster.

1081

Doncaster 1666.

To Traffic 28/3/27.

REPAIRS:
Don. 15/6—22/7/29.**G.**
Don. 21/2—14/5/31.**G.**
Don. 10/5—30/6/34.**G.**
Don. 2/5—18/6/37.**G.**
Don. 2—16/3/40.**G.**
Don. 20/3—10/4/43.**G.**
Don. 6/7—3/8/46.**G.**
Don. 5/12/49—6/1/50.**G.**
Don. 26/1—17/2/53.**G.**
Don. 25/2—17/3/55.**C/L.**
Don. 6/12/56—12/1/57.**G.**
Don. 10/2/60. *Not Repaired.*

BOILERS:
7966 *(new).*
8145 *(exC12 4543)* 14/5/31.
9305 *(new)* 10/4/43.
8515 *(ex8951)* 6/1/50.
21922 *(new)* 17/2/53.
21935 *(new)* 12/1/57.

SHEDS:
Doncaster.
Ardsley 5/5/27.
Immingham 17/8/27.
Ardsley 29/8/39.
Bradford 26/3/41.
Low Moor 12/1/58.

RENUMBERED:
8969 27/1/46.
68969 6/1/50.

CONDEMNED: 22/2/60.
Cut up at Doncaster.

_____

1082

Doncaster 1667.

To Traffic 30/4/27.

REPAIRS:
Don. 3/5—13/6/29.**G.**
Don. 15/4—29/7/32.**G.**
Don. 16/3—13/4/35.**G.**
Don. 19—31/1/38.**G.**
Don. 10/8—31/8/40.**G.**
Don. 30/10—27/11/43.**G.**
Don. 24/11—21/12/46.**G.**
Don. 8/8—2/9/49.**G.**
Don. 18/5—13/6/52.**G.**
Don. 6/1—3/2/55.**G.**
Don. 7/2—1/3/58.**G.**
Don. 19/4/61. *Not Repaired.*

BOILERS:
7967 *(new).*
8150 *(exJ4 4044)* 29/7/32.
8269 *(ex2793)* 31/1/38.
8168 *(exC12 7367)* 21/12/46.
21870 *(reno from 8162)* 13/6/52.
21908 *(exC12 67394)* 3/2/55.
21829 *(ex68933)* 1/3/58.

SHEDS:
Ardsley.
Immingham 19/9/27.
Keadby 23/11/27.
Frodingham 12/6/32.
Doncaster 15/6/58.
Hornsey 26/10/58.

RENUMBERED:
8970 27/1/46.
68970 2/9/49.

CONDEMNED: 19/4/61.
Cut up at Doncaster.

_____

1086

Doncaster 1668.

To Traffic 14/5/27.

REPAIRS:
Don. 27/7—24/8/29.**G.**
Don. 15/1—12/3/32.**G.**
Don. 27/4—16/6/34.**G.**
Don. 30/6—24/7/37.**G.**
Don. 15—20/5/38.**L.**
Spark arrestor fitted.
Don. 30/9—21/10/39.**G.**
Don. 16/5—13/6/42.**G.**
Don. 22/7—5/8/44.**G.**
Don. 7/9—5/10/46.**G.**
Don. 10/11—18/12/48.**G.**
Don. 29/5—22/6/51.**G.**
Str. 28/3—23/4/55.**G.**
Str. 12/2—8/3/58.**C/H.**
Don. 19/10—12/11/60.**G.**
To Service Stock 16/9/62.

BOILERS:
7965 *(new).*
7945 *(ex1058)* 12/3/32.
8320 *(exC12 4545)* 24/7/37.
8170 *(ex8934)* 18/12/48.
21826 *(reno from 8483)* 22/6/51.
21824 *(ex68977)* 23/4/55.
21894 *(ex68913)* 12/11/60.
21894 reno. S.B.4526 16/9/62.

SHEDS:
Ardsley.
Keadby 25/11/27.
Frodingham 12/6/32.
Immingham 15/9/32.
Frodingham 28/7/46.

No.68971 did get its number on bunker changed to No.15 Departmental Locomotive during the works holiday in week ending 14th September 1963. But it kept both its smokebox and shed plate until 30th May 1965 when condemned and later sold for cutting up by T.W.Ward.

No.68976 became No.16 Departmental Locomotive and kept smokebox number plate and 34B Hornsey shed plate which it should have lost on 9th July 1961. Note that it was using one of the special Weigh House lamps. Condemned 30th May 1965 along with the others, it was sold for scrap in July to T.W.Ward. Doncaster works.

The group of seven which worked from Eastfield shed in Glasgow merit special mention for the variety of treatment they got after becoming Nos.8952 to 8958 in April/May 1946. No.8952, ex works 20th June 1947 had LNER restored with that and its number in painted, unshaded Gill sans. From its next 'General', out 12th January 1950, the only painting attention was the blacking over of the 12in. number 8952 and substitution of 68952 in 9in. figures still using modified 6 and 9. Eastfield, 27th September 1952.

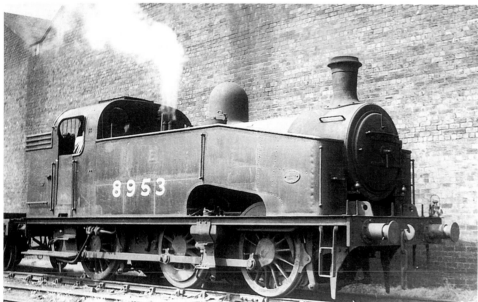

From a repair out 1st September 1945 only NE appeared in 7½in. size but applied by shaded transfers, and from a General repair ex Cowlairs 10th May 1947, this was not altered. No.8953 was put on in normal 12in. shaded transfers. Sighthill, 14th August 1947.

(below) Out 16th October 1948 from a General repair, No.68954 had been fully repainted, with its number moved to the bunker and at 9in. size matching BRITISH RAILWAYS in painted and unshaded characters. At the front, the number was still on the bufferbeam where, as on the bunker, 6 and 9 were not in true Gill sans. Eastfield, 7th November 1948.

From a 'General' on 13th March 1947, No.8955 had 7½in. LNER and 12in. numbers in the shaded transfers which had been standard since 1923. It was out 26th June 1948 from a Light repair changed to its BR number 68955 but still put on in LNER shaded transfers. Eastfield, 21st June 1949.

This was the Cowlairs style when No.8956 was painted after General repair and ex works 31st May 1947. Unshaded 7½in. LNER combined with 12in. widely spaced numbers including modified 6 and 9. But on the bufferbeam the number was still in the 4½in. shaded transfers. Eastfield, 20th March 1948.

1086 cont./
Hornsey 19/10/52.
New England 9/7/61.
Doncaster 3/6/62.
Doncaster Works 16/9/62.

RENUMBERED:
 8971 27/1/46.
 68971 18/12/48.
 DEPT'L No.15 16/9/62.
 Seen 12/11/62 by WBY as 68971.

WITHDRAWN: 16/9/62.
CONDEMNED: 30/5/65.
*Sold for scrap to T.W. Ward,
Beighton, 7/65.*

2789

Doncaster 1732.

To Traffic 22/2/30.

REPAIRS:
Don. 23/4—5/8/32.**G.**
Don. 12/10—3/11/34.**G.**
Don. 30/7—14/8/37.**G.**
Don. 12—22/4/38.**L.**
Spark Arrestor fitted.
Don. 2—16/12/39.**G.**
Don. 10/1—7/2/42.**G.**
Don. 8—29/4/44.**G.**
Don. 2/2—9/3/46.**G.**
Don. 3/7—3/9/48.**G.**
Don. 20—29/12/50.**N/C.**
Don. 23/5—19/6/51.**G.**
Str. 7/12/53—2/1/54.**G.**
Don. 1—29/7/55.**G.**
Don. 11/5—15/7/60.**G.**

BOILERS:
 8265 *(new).*
 7931 *(ex603)* 14/8/37.
 7815 *(ex3237)* 9/3/46.
 9823 *(new)* 3/9/48.
 21825 *(reno from 8548)* 19/6/51.
 21859 *(ex68974)* 29/7/55.
 21935 *(ex68969)* 15/7/60.

SHEDS:
Doncaster.
Immingham 29/3/30.
Annesley 13/10/46.
Colwick 29/2/48.
Hornsey 28/9/52.
Doncaster 9/7/61.

RENUMBERED:
 8972 24/3/46.
 68972 3/9/48.

CONDEMNED: 16/9/62.
Into Don. for cut up 6/11/62.

2790

Doncaster 1734.

To Traffic 22/2/30.

REPAIRS:
Don. 23/5—13/8/32.**G.**
Don. 12/10—3/11/34.**G.**
Don. 14/11—4/12/37.**G.**
Don. 30/4—5/5/38.**L.**
Spark Arrestor fitted.
Don. 9—30/3/40.**G.**
Don. 4—25/4/42.**G.**
Don. 27/5—10/6/44.**G.**
Don. 17/8—7/9/46.**G.**
Don. 20/3—9/4/49.**G.**
Don. 3/9—30/10/51.**H/I.**
Don. 11/5—4/6/54.**G.**
Don. 18/2—23/3/57.**G.**
Don. 21/7/59. *Not Repaired.*

BOILERS:
 8266 *(new).*
 8267 *(ex2791)* 4/12/37.
 8266 *(ex596)* 10/6/44.
 8671 *(ex8928)* 9/4/49.
 8671 reno.21843 30/10/51.
 21950 *(reno from 8686)* 4/6/54.
 21937 *(new)* 23/3/57.

SHEDS:
Doncaster.
Immingham 29/3/30.
Frodingham 29/3/37.
Immingham 5/5/37.
Frodingham 29/12/46.
Doncaster 21/6/53.
Frodingham 20/6/54.
Doncaster 25/1/59.

RENUMBERED:
 8973 14/4/46.
 68973 9/4/49.

CONDEMNED: 21/7/59.
Cut up at Doncaster.

2791

Doncaster 1735.

To Traffic 22/2/30.

REPAIRS:
Don. 25/7—30/9/32.**G.**
Don. 1—20/3/35.**G.**
Don. 29/9—16/10/37.**G.**
Don. 10—17/6/38.**L.**
Park Arrestor fitted.
Don. 17/2—2/3/40.**G.**
Don. 6—27/3/43.**G.**
Don. 15/9—6/10/45.**G.**
Don. 2—30/1/48.**G.**

Don. 2—28/3/52.**G.**
Don. 18/5—11/6/54.**C/L.**
Don. 26/5—1/7/55.**G.**
Don. 30/7/59. *Not Repaired.*

BOILERS:
 8267 *(new).*
 7947 *(ex1079)* 16/10/37.
 9102 *(ex605)* 6/10/45.
 21859 *(reno from 8270)* 28/3/52.
 21854 *(ex68940)* 1/7/55.

SHEDS:
Doncaster.
Immingham 22/4/30.
Frodingham 11/8/46.
Doncaster 28/9/46.
Mexborough 18/12/49.
Frodingham 15/10/50.
Doncaster 21/6/53.
Colwick 2/2/58.

RENUMBERED:
 8974 14/4/46.
 E8974 30/1/48.
 68974 28/3/52.

CONDEMNED: 3/8/59.
Cut up at Doncaster.

2792

Doncaster 1737.

To Traffic 22/2/30.

REPAIRS:
Don. 8/8—14/10/32.**G.**
Don. 13/9—5/10/34.**G.**
Don. 10/5—26/6/37.**G.**
Don. 24—28/6/38.**L.**
Spark Arrestor fitted.
Don. 22/7—19/8/39.**G.**
Don. 13/9—4/10/41.**G.**
Don. 2—23/10/43.**G.**
Don. 12/1—2/2/46.**G.**
Don. 8/3—13/4/48.**G.**
Don. 17/6—20/7/51.**G.**
Don. 7/6—7/7/54.**G.**
Don. 24/4—22/5/58.**G.**
Don. 29/7/61. *Not Repaired.*

BOILERS:
 8268 *(new).*
 9252 *(new)* 4/10/41.
 9310 *(ex8940)* 13/4/48.
 21829 *(reno from 9508)* 20/7/51.
 21843 *(ex68973)* 7/7/54.
 21964 *(ex68977)* 22/5/58.

SHEDS:
Doncaster.
Immingham 23/4/30.
Woodford Halse 19/2/35.

Immingham 16/4/35.
Annesley 25/8/46.
Hornsey 19/10/52.
Annesley 23/11/52.
Hornsey 14/6/53.
Annesley 5/7/53.
Colwick 30/10/55.
Hornsey 14/2/60.
King's Cross 9/7/61.

RENUMBERED:
 8975 14/4/46.
 68975 13/4/48.

CONDEMNED: 29/7/61.
Cut up at Doncaster.

2793

Doncaster 1739.

To Traffic 19/4/30.

REPAIRS:
Don. 5/9—7/11/32.**G.**
Don. 1—20/3/35.**G.**
Don. 14/11—7/12/37.**G.**
Don. 17/3—2/4/38.**L.**
Spark Arrestor fitted.
Don. 30/3—4/5/40.**G.**
*In Summer 1940, LNER charged
the Railway Executive Com-
mittee £25 for "Armouring for
Defensive Purposes in Grimsby/
Immingham Area".*
Don. 3—24/4/43.**G.**
Don. 1—15/9/45.**G.**
Don. 23/10—26/11/47.**G.**
Don. 17/3—20/4/49.**C/H.**
Don. 22/4—18/5/51.**G.**
Don. 22/8—3/9/52.**C/L.**
Don. 16/1—11/2/54.**G.**
Don. 25/3—7/5/57.**G.**
Don. 3—16/7/58.**C/L.**
Don. 22/9—21/10/60.**G.**
To Service Stock 16/9/62.

BOILERS:
 8269 *(new).*
 7928 *(ex593)* 7/12/37.
 8267 *(ex2790)* 15/9/45.
 9307 *(ex8950)* 20/4/49.
 21910 *(new)* 18/5/51.
 21806 *(ex68922)* 11/2/54.
 21803 *(ex68902)* 7/5/57.
 21803 reno. S.B. 4527 16/9/62.

SHEDS:
Doncaster.
Immingham 19/5/30.
Annesley 25/8/46.
Hornsey 19/10/52.
Annesley 23/11/52.
New England 14/12/58.

No.8956 remained as above until ex works 18th February 1950 from a Light repair. LNER was not disturbed but the 12in. 8956 was changed to 68956 in the same style but closer spaced and only 9in. high. At the front, smokebox plate superseded bufferbeam number, and had correct Gill sans included. It remained as shown until ex works 26th April 1953. Eastfield, 6th April 1952.

The 7½in. NE dated from 10th March 1945 heavy repair and when No.635 was changed to 8957 on Sunday 28th April 1946, 12in. figures were painted on. Eastfield, June 1947.

From a General repair on 13th November 1947 No.8957 came out with shaded transfers, 7½in. for LNER and 12in. for 8957. From its next 'General' on 27th May 1950 the LNER was not disturbed but the 68957 was closely spaced and in the 10in. size which had then become standard. Smokebox plate was put on and correct Gill sans figuring was used by the paint shop. Even so, the number was still on the tanks and stayed there (with LNER) until 11th November 1953. Eastfield, 12th June 1950.

Ex works 4th June 1948, Cowlairs put BRITISH RAILWAYS on the same high level as LNER had been but then moved 68958 to the bunker at the same level. Despite so clearly looking wrong, it was not altered when No.68958 was ex works 30th December 1949 but it did then get smokebox number plate as shown in this 26th March 1950 photograph. It remained thus until 20th December 1951. Eastfield, 26th March 1950.

The ten built in 1924 came out new as Nos.3231 to 3240. These and the thirty-two built 1926/7 all had black with red lining which Nos.3221 to 3230 also got when first shopped in 1925/6. From June 1928 only plain black was used, alike for new, existing engines and rebuilds from J51 class (see page 132).

2793 cont./
Hornsey 24/1/60.
New England 9/7/61.
Doncaster 3/6/62.
Doncaster Works 16/9/62.

RENUMBERED:
8976 14/4/46.
68976 20/4/49.
DEPT'L No.16 16/9/62.

WITHDRAWN: 16/9/62.
CONDEMNED: 30/5/65.
*Sold for scrap to T.W. Ward,
Beighton, 7/65.*

2794

Doncaster 1740.

To Traffic 19/4/30.

REPAIRS:
Don. 20/5—4/7/34.**G.**
Don. 28/9—15/10/37.**G.**
Don. 24/2—9/3/40.**G.**
Don. 13—27/6/42.**H/I.**
Don. 14/4—12/5/45.**G.**
Don. 12/9—16/10/48.**G.**
Don. 19/5—11/6/51.**G.**
Str. 26/1—27/2/54.**G.**
Don. 31/3—3/5/58.**G.**

BOILERS:
8270 *(new).*
7926 *(ex591)* 15/10/37.
9312 *(new)* 12/5/45.
21824 *(reno from 8144)* 11/6/51.
21964 *(reno from 9107)* 27/2/54.
21908 *(ex68970)* 3/5/58.

SHEDS:
Doncaster.
Ardsley 23/5/30.
Stratford 14/11/30.
Immingham 29/1/56.
Frodingham 6/1/57.
Doncaster 3/5/59.
Copley Hill 6/8/61.
Low Moor 20/8/61.
Wakefield 23/12/62.

RENUMBERED:
8977 2/6/46.
68977 16/10/48.

CONDEMNED: 23/9/63.
Into Dar. for cut up 10/63.

599

Gorton.

To Traffic 10/11/38.

REPAIRS:
Don. 15—29/7/39.**L.**
Don. 5—19/12/42.**G.**
Don. 6—20/10/45.**G.**
Don. 14/3—22/4/48.**G.**
Don. 25/6—25/7/51.**G.**
Don. 15/12/54—14/1/55.**G.**
Don. 27/7—19/8/57.**C/H.**
Don. 19/11/58. *Not Repaired.*

BOILERS:
9099 *(new).*
21831 *(reno from 9253)* 25/7/51.
21853 *(ex68923)* 14/1/55.

SHEDS:
Ardsley.
Copley Hill 24/11/38.

RENUMBERED:
8978 2/6/46.
68978 22/4/48.

CONDEMNED: 19/11/58.
Cut up at Doncaster.

600

Gorton.

To Traffic 19/11/38.

REPAIRS:
Gor. 8—12/12/38.**L.**
Str. 11—12/5/39.**L.**
Str. 17—21/10/39.**L.**
Don. 15—29/3/41.**G.**
Don. 19/9—3/10/42.**G.**
Don. 5/5—2/6/45.**G.**
Don. 26/11—23/12/47.**G.**
Don. 3—28/8/52.**G.**
Don. 20/8—28/9/56.**G.**
Don. 6/2/61. *Not Repaired.*

BOILERS:
9100 *(new).*
21917 *(new)* 28/8/52.
21872 *(ex68990)* 28/9/56.

SHEDS:
Cambridge.
Stratford 23/3/42.
Doncaster 1/6/46.
Frodingham 27/2/49.
Mexborough 15/10/50.
Immingham 21/6/53.
Hornsey 13/3/55.

RENUMBERED:
8979 13/4/46.
68979 28/8/52.

CONDEMNED: 6/2/61.
Cut up at Doncaster.

602

Gorton.

To Traffic 3/12/38.

REPAIRS:
Don. 5—26/7/41.**G.**
Don. 18/3—1/4/44.**G.**
Don. 17/1—22/2/47.**G.**
Don. 21/9—13/10/50.**G.**
Don. 18/12/54—22/1/55.**G.**
Don. 15/2/60. *Not Repaired.*

BOILERS:
9101 *(new).*
8144 *(ex8901)* 22/2/47.
21804 *(reno fm. 8765)* 13/10/50.
21817 *(ex68926)* 22/1/55.

SHEDS:
Cambridge.
Stratford 18/12/38.
Doncaster 12/3/46.
Mexborough 11/11/51.
Frodingham 17/5/53.
Doncaster 20/5/56.
Hornsey 26/10/58.

RENUMBERED:
8980 2/6/46.
68980 13/10/50.

CONDEMNED: 22/2/60.
Cut up at Doncaster.

605

Gorton.

To Traffic 17/12/38.

REPAIRS:
Gor. 16—18/2/39.**L.**
Don. 27/9—18/10/41.**G.**
Don. 22/1—5/2/44.**G.**
Don. 13/7—3/8/46.**G.**
Don. 3—30/8/48.**G.**
Don. 9/7—7/8/52.**G.**
Don. 11/2—21/3/57.**G.**
Don. 5/2—19/3/60.**C/L.**
Don. 19/4/61. *Not Repaired.*

BOILERS:
9102 *(new).*

9311 *(new)* 5/2/44.
9822 *(new)* 30/8/48.
21876 *(reno from 9312)* 7/8/52.
21923 *(ex68959)* 21/3/57.

SHEDS:
Colwick.
Leicester 27/11/49.
Colwick 14/9/52.
Hornsey 19/10/52.

RENUMBERED:
8981 20/1/46.
68981 30/8/48.

CONDEMNED: 19/4/61.
Cut up at Doncaster.

606

Gorton.

To Traffic 31/12/38.

REPAIRS:
Don. 9—30/11/40.**G.**
Don. 28/11—12/12/42.**G.**
Don. 9—30/12/44.**G.**
Don. 5/2—8/3/47.**G.**
Don. 5—26/5/49.**G.**
Don. 5—30/5/52.**G.**
Don. 29/8—4/10/56.**G.**
Don. 3/8—2/9/60.**G.**

BOILERS:
9103 *(new).*
9304 *(new)* 12/12/42.
9308 *(new)* 30/12/44.
9306 *(ex8947)* 26/5/49.
21868 *(reno from 9112)* 30/5/52.
21878 *(ex68991)* 4/10/56.

SHEDS:
Colwick.
Annesley 2/2/39.
Colwick 13/7/47.
Hornsey 19/10/52.
Lincoln 9/7/61.
Colwick 22/10/61.
Doncaster 10/6/62.

RENUMBERED:
8982 16/6/46.
68982 26/5/49.

CONDEMNED: 16/9/62.
Into Don. for cut up 6/11/62.

(*above*) Starting 22nd August 1942 with No.3231, only NE was put on but 12in. shaded transfers were used.

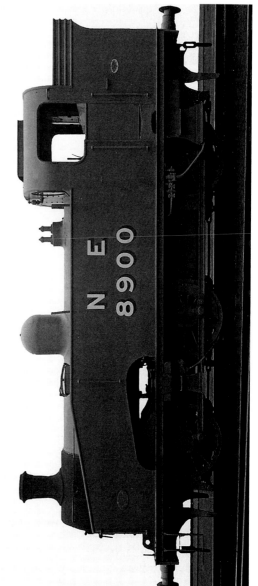

The 1946 renumbering scheme had been drawn up in 1943. As early as 4th April 1944 No.2789 had been painted grey on the left side only and renumbered 8900, with the wartime lettering NE. This was not its correct number under the scheme and the engine re-entered traffic painted black and with its old number. The reason for this temporary renumbering was to obtain a photograph of this and various other classes for Thompson's dossier on standard engine classes.

Use of the large NE overlapped the 1946 renumbering in which the class took numbers 8890 to 8991. No.587 had 12in NE ex works 8th December 1945 but on Sunday 17th March 1946 Copley Hill shed changed it to 8988 using 7½in. stencils, thus reversing the standard of 7½in. letters and 12in. numbers.

From January 1946, LNER in normal 7½in. shaded transfers was restored and many combined this with unshaded 7½in. stencilled renumbering. Bradford shed applied number 8897, in place of 3187, on Sunday 24th November 1946, the LNER dating from ex works 11th May 1946.

608

Gorton.

To Traffic 28/1/39.

REPAIRS:
Don. 7—21/11/42.**G.**
Don. 1—22/9/45.**G.**
Don. 15—22/8/47.**N/C.**
For painting & photograph.
Don. 9/11—10/12/47.**G.**
Don. 6/6—6/7/50.**G.**
Str. 31/12/52—12/2/53.**G.**
Str. 2/6—20/8/57.**G.**
Str. 8/4—8/5/58.**C/L.**
Don. 23/3—7/5/60.**C/H.**
Don. 24/4/62. *Not Repaired.*

BOILERS:
9104 *(new).*
9109 *(ex8950)* 6/7/50.
21960 *(reno from 9105)* 12/2/53.
21950 *(ex68898)* 7/5/60.

SHEDS:
Doncaster.
Sheffield 13/2/40.
Hornsey 19/10/52.
Doncaster 9/7/61.

RENUMBERED:
8983 14/4/46.
68983 6/7/50.

CONDEMNED: 24/4/62.
Cut up at Doncaster.

611

Gorton.

To Traffic 18/2/39.

REPAIRS:
Don. 28/9—19/10/40.**L.**
Don. 6—20/3/43.**G.**
Don. 20/7—17/8/46.**G.**
Don. 21/2—22/3/49.**G.**
Don. 17/12/51—9/1/52.**G.**
Don. 30/7—23/8/54.**G.**
Don. 13—16/9/55.**N/C.**
Don. 15/2—14/3/57.**G.**
Don. 5—31/10/59.**G.**

BOILERS:
9105 *(new).*
21851 *(reno from 9824)* 9/1/52.
21846 *(ex68962)* 23/8/54.
21947 *(ex68988)* 14/3/57.

SHEDS:
Doncaster.
Copley Hill 6/2/40.

RENUMBERED:
8984 2/6/46.
68984 22/3/49.

CONDEMNED: 25/3/63.
Into Don. for cut up 8/4/63.

615

Gorton.

To Traffic 1/4/39.

REPAIRS:
Str. 16—23/7/39.**L.**
Str. 12—23/2/40.**L.**
Don. 2—23/11/40.**L.**
Don. 26/7—23/8/41.**G.**
Don. 5—26/8/44.**G.**
Don. 1/5—3/6/47.**G.**
Don. 8/12/50—2/1/51.**L/I.**
Don. 27/2—9/3/51.**C/L.**
Don. 8/8—17/9/55.**G.**
Don. 14/11/59. *Not Repaired.*

BOILERS:
9106 *(new).*
9106 *reno.21814 2/1/51.*
21850 *(ex68950)* 17/9/55.

SHEDS:
Norwich.
Stratford 30/5/41.
Doncaster 29/3/46.
Hornsey 19/10/52.

RENUMBERED:
8985 7/7/46.
68985 2/1/51.

CONDEMNED: 16/11/59.
Cut up at Doncaster.

584

Gorton.

To Traffic 29/4/39.

REPAIRS:
Don. 15—29/11/41.**G.**
Don. 29/7—12/8/44.**G.**
Don. 5/7—17/8/47.**G.**
Don. 24/7—21/8/51.**G.**
Don. 24/7—19/8/55.**G.**
Don. 8/10—4/11/59.**G.**
Don. 2/7/62. *Not Repaired.*

BOILERS:
9107 *(new).*
21835 *(reno from 9310)* 21/8/51.
21862 *(ex68896)* 19/8/55.
21800 *(ex C12 67394)* 4/11/59.

SHEDS:
Stratford.
Doncaster 14/7/46.
Hornsey 19/10/52.
Doncaster 9/7/61.

RENUMBERED:
8986 1/6/46.
68986 21/8/51.

CONDEMNED: 2/7/62.
Cut up at Doncaster.

585

Gorton.

To Traffic 20/5/39.

REPAIRS:
Don. 14—28/8/43.**G.**
Don. 28/9—19/10/46.**G.**
Don. 11/10—4/11/49.**G.**
Str. 27/10—28/11/53.**G.**
Str. 14—28/2/57.**N/C.**
Don. 5/12/58—10/1/59.**G.**
Don. 24/4/62. *Not Repaired.*

BOILERS:
9108 *(new).*
9249 *(ex8909)* 4/11/49.
21963 *(reno fm. 9109)* 28/11/53.
21946 *(ex68946)* 10/1/59.

SHEDS:
Hornsey.
King's Cross 21/4/40.
Gorton 27/3/41.
Trafford Park 23/4/41.
Gorton 30/7/41.
Doncaster 31/5/43.
Hornsey 19/10/52.
Doncaster 9/7/61.

RENUMBERED:
8987 17/3/46.
68987 4/11/49.

CONDEMNED: 24/4/62.
Cut up at Doncaster.

587

Gorton.

To Traffic 10/6/39.

REPAIRS:
Don. 28/11—12/12/42.**G.**
Don. 3/11—8/12/45.**G.**
Don. 4/10—12/11/48.**G.**
Don. 17/7—13/8/51.**G.**
Don. 22/3—14/4/54.**G.**

Don. 18/1—15/2/57.**G.**
Don. 18—28/1/58.**N/C.**
Don. 9/11—10/12/59.**G.**

BOILERS:
9109 *(new).*
9112 *(ex8991)* 12/11/48.
21834 *(reno from 8170)* 13/8/51.
21947 *(reno from 9304)* 14/4/54.
21868 *(ex68982)* 15/2/57.

SHEDS:
Hornsey.
Hitchin 11/6/39.
Trafford Park 28/7/40.
Doncaster 31/5/43.
Ardsley 18/12/43.
Copley Hill 31/12/43.

RENUMBERED:
8988 17/3/46.
68988 12/11/48.

CONDEMNED: 23/9/63.
Into Dar. for cut up 11/63.

590

Gorton.

To Traffic 7/7/39.

REPAIRS:
Don. 10—24/10/42.**G.**
Don. 21/7—18/8/45.**G.**
Don. 5/5—9/6/48.**G.**
Don. 3—28/2/52.**G.**
Don. 25/9—19/10/56.**G.**
Don. 30/1—2/3/60.**G.**

BOILERS:
9110 *(new).*
9825 *(new)* 9/6/48.
21857 *(reno from 9099)* 28/2/52.
21867 *(ex68917)* 19/10/56.
21807 *(ex68922)* 2/3/60.

SHEDS:
Doncaster.
Sheffield 15/8/39.
Doncaster 14/5/42.
Hornsey 19/10/52.
New England 2/7/61.
Doncaster 3/6/62.

RENUMBERED:
8989 31/3/46.
68989 9/6/48.

CONDEMNED: 11/7/62.
Into Don. for cut up 11/7/62.

At the first subsequent works visit, the renumbering was tidied up into standard 7½in. letters and 12in. numbers applied by shaded transfers. No.1058 had been altered to 8962 by Immingham shed on Sunday 27th January 1946, ex Doncaster works 22nd June 1946 it was as shown in this photograph taken that day.

On Saturday 1st June 1946 at Stratford shed No.584 was renumbered 8986 in 12in. shaded transfers. Dirt obscured the company initials but these would be 12in. NE put on 12th August 1944.

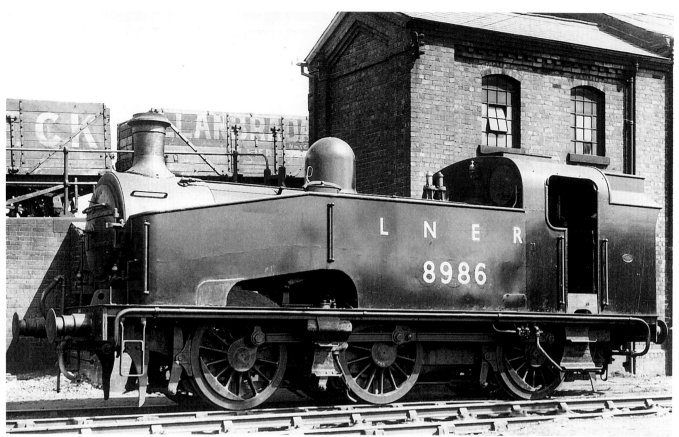

From a General repair No.8986 was ex Doncaster works on 17th August 1947 with LNER restored but in painted and unshaded Gill sans. Numbers were similar but 12in. and they had the LNER modified 6 and 9. Doncaster.

One J50 participated in the 1946 decision to repaint to green all classes except A4 and W1. Ex works 6th November 1946, No.8891 had pre-war green paint with full black and white lining but it reverted to unlined black when it next went to works on 15th August 1949.

595

Gorton.

To Traffic 29/7/39.

REPAIRS:
Don. 9—30/5/42.**G**.
Don. 5—26/8/44.**G**.
Don. 23/2—1/4/47.**G**.
Don. 9—27/5/49.**C/L**.
Don. 3—24/11/49.**G**.
Don. 27/5—20/6/52.**G**.
Don. 22/7—22/8/56.**G**.
Don. 21/4/61. *Not Repaired.*

BOILERS:
9111 *(new)*.
8446 *(ex8916)* 1/4/47.
9108 *(ex8987)* 24/11/49.
21872 *(reno from 9311)* 20/6/52.
21904 *(exC12 67364)* 22/8/56.

SHEDS:
Doncaster.
Sheffield 11/9/39.
Hornsey 19/10/52.

RENUMBERED:
8990 14/4/46.
68990 27/5/49.

CONDEMNED: 21/4/61.
Cut up at Doncaster.

598

Gorton.

To Traffic 26/8/39.

REPAIRS:
Don. 30/1—20/2/43.**G**.
Don. 29/12/45—26/1/46.**G**.
Don. 30/9—29/10/48.**G**.
Don. 12/8—4/9/52.**G**.
Don. 6/6—19/7/56.**G**.
Don. 2/11—2/12/60.**G**.
Don. 30/8/61. *Not Repaired.*

BOILERS:
9112 *(new)*.
9110 *(ex8989)* 29/10/48.
21878 *(reno from 9822)* 4/9/52.
21851 *(exC12 67384)* 19/7/56.
21938 *(ex68902)* 2/12/60.

SHEDS:
Doncaster.
Hornsey 28/9/52.
King's Cross 9/7/61.

RENUMBERED:
8991 31/3/46.
68991 29/10/48.

CONDEMNED: 30/8/61.
Cut up at Doncaster.

(below) **By 16th January 1948 Doncaster were already showing the changed ownership, and with it, they moved the number from tank to bunker. Between 16th January and 12th March 1948, eight Nos.8909, 8914, 8921, 8926, 8927, 8929, 8938 and 8974, got this style with E prefix added to their number. Ardsley, August 1948.**

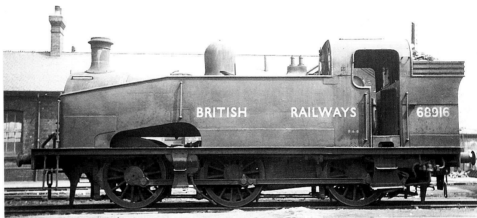

Beginning on 19th March 1948 with No.68940 the full BR number was put on but using the modified 6 and 9 as on 68916, ex works 28th January 1949. Ardsley, June 1949.

By 18th March 1949 when No.68928 was ex works, correct Gill sans 6 and 9 were being used. Darnall, 2nd July 1950.

The **BRITISH RAILWAYS** lettering ceased to be used from August 1949 but for a short while transfers for the BR emblem were awaited. No.68967, ex works 28th September 1949, was one which went back into traffic with plain tanks. Cambridge, 28th September 1949.

By the end of October 1949, the emblem was being applied in the smaller (15½in.) size. It was handed to point to the front on both sides. Doncaster shed, 17th June 1956.

(below) The larger bunkers could have the number centrally placed.

From April 1957 the BR crest superseded the emblem and it too was handed, so on the right hand side the lion faced to the right and this was a serious breach of heraldic rules. Stratford, October 1966.

(above) Engines painted in 1959 and later did have the correct crest applied on their right hand side. Doncaster, 26th September 1959.

General repairs were still made almost to the end of 1960, No.68991 ex works 2nd December 1960 being the last, so a good proportion got the BR crest. King's Cross, 30th December 1960.

J84 No.1 entered Doncaster plant on 9th February 1924 and emerged as LNER 3112 on 5th July in black with single red lining. The only alteration was a change of position for the brass plate showing E&WYUR No.1 which, curiously, was re-fixed on the cab side panel, allowing transfers to be put on the tank. At this shopping, both letters and numbers were 7½ inch size

No.3112. had one more general repair at Doncaster from 25th October to 20th December 1928 and some detail alterations were made, The original built-up chimney was replaced by a shorter GNR pattern. The handrail which curved up and over the smokebox was cut into three short horizontal parts, a knob was fitted on the smokebox door and the brass plate was taken off the cab side. The red lining disappeared but the number was now put on in 12 inch figures. No.3112 was withdrawn 14th June 1930 making Class J84 extinct.

When No.2 got the more substantial frames in 1915, they did not have lightening holes between the leading and middle axle boxes. The 6 inch longer front overhang led to that end being cut at a straight slant instead of a curve. From Doncaster on 15th November 1924 it was black with red lining as LNER 3113, also having 7½ inch figures and having lost the No.2 brass plate. Although in Doncaster again 24th January to 25th April 1928, it was withdrawn on 22nd December 1928, but only cut up in May 1929.

CLASS J84

3112 (E&WYUR No.1)

Manning Wardle 1307

To traffic 6/1895.

REPAIRS:
MW. ?/?—?/4/14.**G.**
Don. 9/2—5/7/24.**G.**
Don. 5/3—26/6/26.**L.**
Don. 6—28/8/26.**L.**
Don. 25/10—20/12/28.**G.**

BOILERS:
1.
1 *(new)* ?/4/14.

SHEDS:
Robin Hood
Ardsley ?/7/26.

RENUMBERED:
3112 5/7/24.

CONDEMNED: 14/6/30.
Cut up at Doncaster.

3113 (E&WYUR No.2)

Manning Wardle 1308.

To traffic 7/1895.

REPAIRS:
MW. ?/?—?/3/16.**G.**
Don. 3/9—15/11/24.**G.**
Don. 24/1—25/4/28.**G.**

BOILERS:
2.
2 *(new)* ?/3/16.

SHEDS:
Robin Hood.
Ardsley ?/7/26.

RENUMBERED:
3113 15/11/24.

CONDEMNED: 22/12/28.
Cut up at Doncaster.

E&WYUR No.3

Manning Wardle 1489.

To traffic 9/1900.

REPAIRS:
MW. ?/?—?/6/11.**G.**

BOILERS:
3.
3 *(new)* ?/6/11.

SHED:
Robin Hood.

CONDEMNED: 6/9/23.
Cut up at Doncaster.

CLASS J85

3114 (E&WYUR No.4)

Manning Wardle 1398.

To traffic 9/1898.

REPAIRS:
MW. ?/?—?/8/19.**G.**
Rebuilt from 0-6-2T.
Ard. 3/3—17/4/24.**L.**
Ard. 27/6—23/8/24.**L.**
Don. 15/6—3/10/25.**G.**
Don. 15/6—13/7/29.**G.**

BOILERS:
4.
4 *(new)* ?/4/19.

SHEDS:
Robin Hood.
Ardsley ?/7/26.

RENUMBERED:
3114 3/10/25.

CONDEMNED: 20/2/33.
Cut up at Doncaster.

From its 15th June to 13th July 1929 residence inside Doncaster shops, appreciable modifications were made to No.3114 as it acquired items from the withdrawn No.3113. It got the 150 gallon smaller tank and the different smokebox door, including wheel and handle, also the front buffers from 3113. It was now in unlined black and had three short handrails at the front end instead of the curved continuous type. The smaller saddle tank dispensed with the handrail over it, leaving only the vertical portion on the right hand side. No.3114 was withdrawn 20th February 1933 clearing Class J85.

Another engine built in August 1898 at Melton Constable as M&GN No 1A was also renumbered in 1907 to become No.93. Melton Constable, 23rd October 1936.

(above) Two further engines, built at Melton Constable in April 1899 and December 1899, Nos.11A and 3A respectively, were renumbered 96 and 95 in 1907. This is No.96 as taken over by LNER.

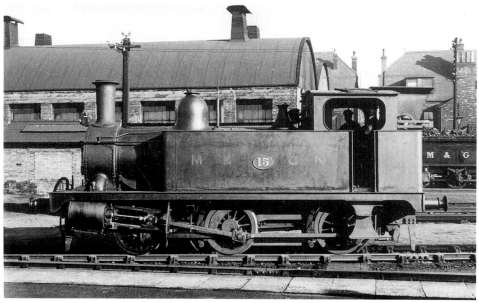

Though building was somewhat slow and infrequent, the 0-6-0 tank engines continued to be turned out by Melton Constable and in January 1901 No.15 appeared. Yarmouth Beach, 24th October 1936.

CLASS J 93

098

Melton Constable 1.

To traffic 10/1897.

REPAIRS:
Str. ?/?—7/8/37.**G.**
Str. ?/?—24/2/43.**G.**
Not in use for 136 days in 1944.
Not in use for 187 days in 1945.

BOILERS:
98.
95 *(ex 95)* 7/8/37.

SHEDS:
South Lynn *at* 1/10/36.
Melton Constable 8/1/38.
South Lynn 19/3/38.
King's Lynn Sept/Oct 1939.
South Lynn 16/4/40.

RENUMBERED:
 098 7/8/37.
 8482 10/8/46.

CONDEMNED: 23/1/47.
Cut up at Stratford.

093

Melton Constable 2.

To traffic 8/1898.

REPAIRS:
Str. ?/?—13/12/37.**G.**
Str. ?/?—28/11/42.**G.**

BOILERS:
 93.
100 *(ex4-4-0T 9A) circa* 1936.
015 *(ex 15)* 13/12/37.

SHEDS:
Melton Constable *at* 1/10/36.
Yarmouth Beach 17/12/37.
Melton Constable 24/1/40.
Yarmouth Beach 8/6/41.
Melton Constable 2/11/41.
Yarmouth Beach 22/2/42.

RENUMBERED:
 093 13/12/37.
 8483 allocated.

CONDEMNED: 9/6/44.
Cut up at Stratford.

096

Melton Constable 3.

To traffic 4/1899.

REPAIRS:
Str. ?/?—10/3/37.**G.**
Str. ?/?—9/12/40.**G.**
Str. ?/?—29/7/44.**G.**
Str. 11/5/48. *Not repaired.*

BOILER:
96.

SHED:
South Lynn *at* 1/10/36.

RENUMBERED:
 096 10/3/37.
 8484 10/8/46.

CONDEMNED: 20/5/48.
Cut up at Stratford.

095

Melton Constable 4.

To traffic 12/1899.

REPAIRS:
Str. ?/?—29/5/37.**G.**
Str. ?/?—16/12/41.**G.**
Str. ?/?—13/11/44.**G.**
Str. 20/12/47. *Not repaired*

BOILERS:
95.
93 *(ex 93)* 29/5/37.

SHED:
South Lynn *at* 1/10/36.

RENUMBERED:
 095 29/5/37.
 8485 10/8/46.

CONDEMNED: 31/12/47.
Cut up at Darlington 5/48.

Two more engines, built March and December 1902 at Melton Constable, Nos.17A and 12A, were later renumbered 99 and 97 by the M&GN. Norwich, 23rd October 1936.

015

Melton Constable 5.

To traffic 1/1901.

REPAIRS:
Str. ?/?—22/11/37.**G.**
Str. ?/?—2/9/42.**G.**

BOILERS:
15.
98 *(ex 98)* 22/11/37.

SHEDS:
Yarmouth Beach *at* 1/10/36.
Melton Constable 15/12/37.
Yarmouth Beach 21/5/44.

RENUMBERED:
015 22/11/37.
8486 allocated.

CONDEMNED: 15/12/45.
Cut up at Stratford.

_____

099

Melton Constable 6.

To traffic 3/1902.

REPAIRS:
Str. ?/?—2/3/37.**G.**
Str. ?/?—16/11/39.**L.**
After collision.
Str. ?/?—6/1/42.**G.**

BOILER:
99.

SHEDS:
Melton Constable *at* 1/10/36.
Yarmouth Beach 5/12/39.
Melton Constable 1/4/40.

RENUMBERED:
099 2/3/37.
8487 allocated.

CONDEMNED: 9/7/45.
Cut up at Stratford.

_____

097

Melton Constable 7.

To traffic 12/1902.

REPAIRS:
Str. ?/?—24/2/38.**G.**
Str. ?/5—30/5/42.**L.**
Damaged by enemy action 23/5/42.

BOILER:
97.

SHEDS:
Melton Constable *at* 1/10/36.
Yarmouth Beach 17/12/37.
Melton Constable 29/5/38.

RENUMBERED:
097 24/2/38.

CONDEMNED: 22/3/43.
Cut up at Stratford.

_____

094

Melton Constable 8.

To traffic 1/1904.

REPAIRS:
Str. ?/?—24/12/37.**G.**
Str. ?/?—5/6/41.**G.**
Str. ?/?—21/10/44.**G.**
Str. 27/12/47. *Not repaired.*

BOILER:
94.

SHED:
South Lynn.

RENUMBERED:
094 24/12/37.
8488 10/8/46.

CONDEMNED: 13/1/48.
Cut up at Darlington 5/48.

_____

016

Melton Constable 9.

To traffic 5/1905.

REPAIRS:
MC. ?/?—?/4/35.**G.**

Str. 4/1—24/5/38.**G.**
Str. 19/6—21/8/42.**G.**
Str. 20/9—8/12/45.**G.**
Str. 4/8/49. *Not repaired.*

BOILER:
16.
16 reno.016 24/5/38.

SHEDS:
Yarmouth Beach *at* 1/10/36.
Melton Constable 17/12/37.
Yarmouth Beach 29/5/38.
Melton Constable 8/10/39.
Yarmouth Beach 1/4/40.
Melton Constable 16/5/43.

RENUMBERED:
016 24/5/38.
8489 21/12/46.

CONDEMNED: 29/8/49.
Cut up at Stratford.

_____

(below) **No.94 started life as M&GN No.2ᴀ as turned out by Melton Constable works in January 1904. It too was renumbered in 1907 and is seen at Melton on 23rd October 1936.**

The final engine which made up the J93 class was built in May 1905 at Melton Constable and, like No.15, managed to keep its original number 16 as here at Yarmouth, 23rd October 1936.

(below) When the nine engines became LNER, only one No.096, retained the smokebox door which was flush fitting and had a plate hinge instead of two straps. It was also the only one still with a continuous boiler handrail. It duly lost both, either at the December 1940 or July 1944 repair by Stratford.

By take-over the other eight engines already had that Johnson door replaced by a Deeley pattern which was more dished, had two hinge straps and clamps instead of central fastening. With that type of door there were handrails in three portions, those on the side were cut to finish level with the front of the smokebox, and a straight short rail was fitted to the door above the upper hinge strap, but also *see* page 195, top.

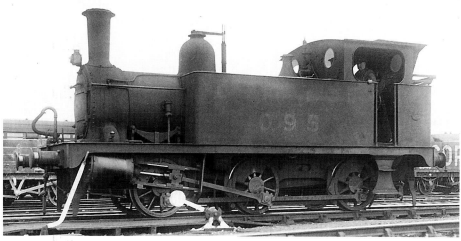

Four of the nine engines inherited wheels which had begun life in 1874 on engines built for the Cornwall Minerals Railway and which were sold in 1880/1 to the Lynn & Fakenham Railway which later became part of the Eastern & Midlands Railway and which was then absorbed by the M&GN on 1st July 1893. These old wheels could be recognised because they had only ten spokes and the balance weights were the built-up type. No.095 kept such wheels to its 31st December 1947 withdrawal. South Lynn.

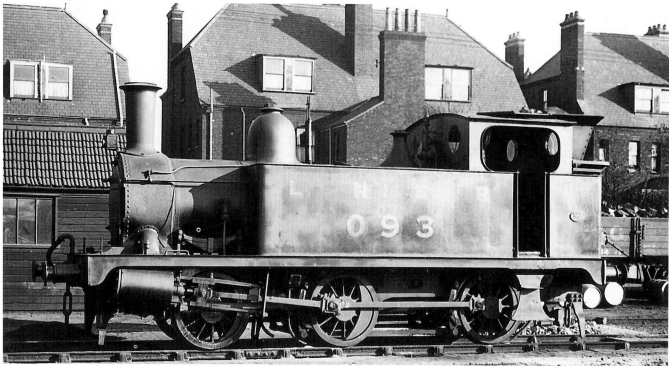

(above) Those engines provided with new wheels, either when built or as replacements, got twelve spoke wheels with crescent shaped balance weights cast into them.

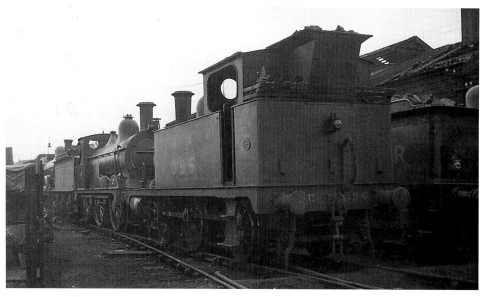

Between 1930 and 1934 all nine tank engines had a hopper put on their bunker to ease coaling from the new mechanical plants installed at South Lynn and Yarmouth Beach sheds. All the engines had two open coal rails and these were never plated. South Lynn, 16th May 1937.

When built, the small ejector in the cab had to serve as the blower but before take-over a separate blower had been fitted on all nine. It was worked by the small bore steam pipe above tank top to smokebox. To provide clearance for the smokebox door to open, the front standpipe for the vacuum train brake was on a swivel connection, but only Nos.095 and 099 still had this type when they became LNER. On the other seven a shorter pipe, fixed on the front of the buffer beam, gave clearance - *see* page 187. Melton Constable, 28th May 1937.

Those engines shopped after July 1942 - which was all except Nos.097 and 099 - got only NE and that was their final designation, because none had LNER restored. Cambridge, 21st January 1945.

In the Thompson re-numbering they were allocated Nos.8482-8489, No.097 having already gone through damage by enemy action at Norwich 23rd May 1942. Further withdrawals led to only Nos.8482, 8484, 8485, 8488 and 8489 taking up their new numbers in 1946. Until the 1939 War they had vacuum brakes for train working and the engine had steam controlled by the vacuum, with the large ejector just to the rear of the smokebox. Nos.8484, 8485 and 8488 at least had train brake piping taken off during the war. South Lynn, 15th August 1946.

No.095, which became 8485, suffered two set-backs to its chimney style. From Stratford, 13th November 1944, it returned with a stove pipe fixed on the base of its cast chimney, but of about the same height. It still had this chimney on 10th August 1946 when it was re-numbered. South Lynn, 15th August 1946.

Some time after 15th August 1946, No.8485 had a short stovepipe chimney fitted, still on the original base, because this is how it arrived at Stratford for repair on 20th December 1947. However, it was instead withdrawn on the 31st. Stratford works, March 1948.

No.016 was renumbered 8489 on Saturday 21st December 1946 at Melton Constable shed although on 15th April 1947 it still had 016 on its rear buffer beam and was also carrying a standpipe for train braking by vacuum. It was the last J93 to have a repair, being ex Stratford 8th December 1945 from a General.

Subsequent to April 1947, when it still had a full cast chimney - see previous illustration - corrosion caused it to lose its top. Note No.8489 retained its train pipe connections for vacuum braking.

When No.8489 arrived at Stratford on 4th August 1949 for examination, the chimney had wasted away even more, and it had also had the coal hopper taken off. It was not considered to be worth repairing and its withdrawal on 29th August 1949 made J93 class extinct. Although with twelve spoke wheels, note the cast-in balance weight on the middle wheel but a built-up type on rear wheel. Stratford, August 1949.

After its final repair in July 1944, No.096/8484's chimney appears to have been a stovepipe, which became somewhat ragged before its 20th May 1948 withdrawal. This was like 8485 in having its train brake piping taken off.

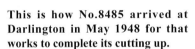

This is how No.8485 arrived at Darlington in May 1948 for that works to complete its cutting up.

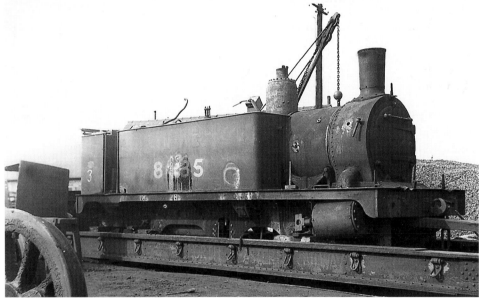

No.8488 also went to Darlington for scrapping in May 1948 but made a more dignified exit. Apart from losing the train brake piping, it was still complete as when it became LNER including a whole cast chimney. Nos.8482, 8484 and 8489 were cut up at Stratford.

CLASS N 19

3115 (E&WYUR No.5)

Manning Wardle 1433.

To traffic 5/1899.

REPAIRS:
Ard. 1—31/5/24.**L.**
Don. 15/12/24—13/3/25.**G.**

BOILER:
5.

SHEDS:
Robin Hood
Ardsley ?/7/26.

RENUMBERED:
3115 13/3/25.

CONDEMNED: 1/3/28.
Cut up at Doncaster.

E&WYUR No.6

Manning Wardle 1434.

To traffic 6/1899.

REPAIRS:
*Not known but none under
LNER.*

BOILER:
6.

SHED:
Robin Hood

CONDEMNED: 6/9/23.
Cut up at Doncaster.

(below) **No.5 went to Doncaster on 15th December 1924 for a General repair and came out on 13th March 1925 as LNER 3115.**

(bottom) **Other than repainting it in unlined black, Doncaster made no alteration to it. It continued to work on its parent line until withdrawn on 1st March 1928 making Class N19 extinct.**

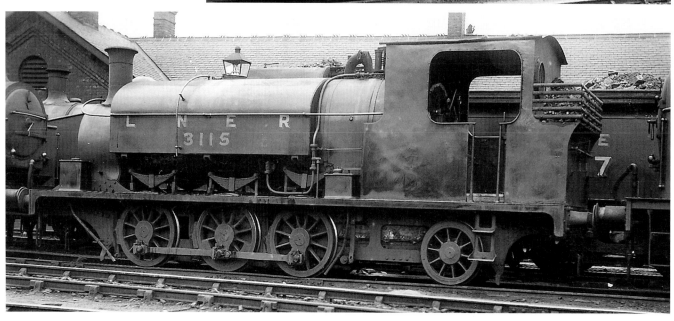